America in God's World

America in God's World

Theology, Ethics, and the Crises
of Bases Abroad, Bad Money, and Black Gold

KENNETH L. VAUX

WIPF & STOCK · Eugene, Oregon

AMERICA IN GOD'S WORLD
Theology, Ethics, and the Crises of Bases Abroad, Bad Money, and Black Gold

Wipf & Stock
A Division of Wipf and Stock Publishers
199 W. 8th Ave., Suite 3
Eugene, OR 97401

www.wipfandstock.com

ISBN 13: 978-1-60608-532-5

Manufactured in the U.S.A.

All scripture citations are adapted from the Authorized King James Version.

I extend a heartfelt thank you to the members of my pastor working group at First Presbyterian Church of Evanston: Terry Halliday, Christopher Miller, Don Wagner and K. K. Yeo. Thanks also to Melanie Baffes, project editor and teaching assistant for the course in which I introduced this book.

As always, Dr. Sara Anson Vaux has been a partner in the substance and style of this work. Thanks to her and to the entire household, down to the tiniest theologian.

Contents

Foreword by Rosemary Radford Ruether ix

INTRODUCTION 1

1 CRISIS IN THE LAND 7

Security

Bases Around the World

American Exceptionalism

The Bush Agenda

Economy

Bad Money

Economic Bubbles and Greed

Global Ripples

Ecology

Black Gold

Ecological Degradation

A Sustainable Future

2 CONTOURS OF A DEFICIENT THEOLOGY AND ETHICS 32

Security

Imperialism

Hegemony

A Chosen People

Economy

Radical Religion

The Invisible Hand

Spreading the Wealth

Ecology
    Lust for Destruction
    Tribulation
    The End of the World

3   CREATIVE THEOLOGY AND THE PROMISE
      OF A BETTER FUTURE 69

Security
    A Theology of Nations

Economy
    A Theology of Economics

Ecology
    A Theology of the Land

4   CONSTRUCTIVE THEOLOGICAL
      AND ETHICAL DIRECTIONS 119

Security
    A New Politics
    Global Reciprocity
    A New World Order

Economy
    A New Global Economy

Ecology
    A New Ecology

    Discussion and Study Guide 153
    Bibliography 155

Foreword

IN *AMERICA IN GOD's World*, Kenneth Vaux continues his decades-long project of seeking an interfaith basis for a theology to undergird justice, health, and peace in God's world. Here, instead of American exceptionalism, Vaux seeks cooperative reciprocity of nations. Instead of a security state, he seeks understanding and human rights in America and worldwide. Instead of hegemony, invasion, and occupation, he seeks the building of a creative community of nations through mutual service. Instead of exclusive faiths negating one another, he seeks the mutual understanding of interfaith cooperation. Instead of furious and destructive global economic competition, he seeks the redevelopment of local economies. And instead of savage exploitation of land, water, and air, he seeks a gentle synergy of human endeavors within our sister earth and all creation.

This is a book that makes a decisive critique of destructive relations of military, economic, and ecological relationships among nations and their fallacious theological and ideological justifications. It also rebuilds theological and ethical supports for a just and sustainable understanding of security, the economy, and human relationship to the environment. Vaux offers a helpful discussion and study guide to enable readers to grapple with these issues and make them their own.

Rosemary Radford Ruether
Claremont Graduate University and School of Theology

Introduction

NOVEMBER 5, 2008. THE most intriguing and perhaps important election in my seventy-year lifetime—the Obama landslide, accumulating some 365 electoral votes—has stunned the nation and thrilled the world. Perhaps the years of doubt by the world's nations concerning America's integrity and credibility and their fear of her international exploits are over. Perhaps a new day is about to dawn. In his Grant Park acceptance speech on November 4, 2008, Obama offered such hope to the home front and to people around the globe:

> . . . to all those watching tonight from beyond our shores…a new dawn of American leadership is at hand. To those who would tear the world down: We will defeat you. To those who seek peace and security: We support you. And to all those who have wondered if America's beacon still burns as bright: Tonight we proved once more that the true strength of our nation comes not from the might of our arms or the scale of our wealth but from the enduring power of our ideals: democracy, liberty, opportunity, and unyielding hope.[1]

Such encouragement, of course, arises against the backdrop of animosity and political chicanery that marked the campaign—reflecting the geopolitical, economic, and cultural turmoil in the world. It also hits up against the harsh realities of the human condition. Where can we look for a livable quotient of hope and realism? In many cases, the global perplexities have been measured against the shaky underpinnings of an uncertain theology.

Former Secretary of State Colin Powell reflected the tension between turmoil and hope in his "Meet the Press" endorsement of Obama. He reacted to the charge that Obama was a Muslim and told a simple tale of a U.S. soldier who gave his life for his country:

---

1. Barack Obama, "This is Your Victory" Acceptance Speech, November 4, 2008, Chicago, Illinois.

... the correct answer is, he is not a Muslim; he's a Christian. He's always been a Christian. But the really right answer is, "what if he is?" Is there something wrong with being a Muslim in this country? The answer's "no, that's not America." I feel strongly about this particular point because of a picture I saw in a magazine. It was a photo essay about troops who are serving in Iraq and Afghanistan. And one picture at the tail end of this photo essay was of a mother in Arlington cemetery, and she had her head on the headstone of her son's grave. And as the picture focused in, you could see the writing on the headstone. And it gave his awards—Purple Heart, Bronze Star—showed that he had died in Iraq, gave his date of birth, date of death. He was twenty years old. And then, at the very top of the headstone, it didn't have a Christian cross. It didn't have the Star of David; it had a crescent and a star of the Islamic faith. And his name was Kareem Rashad Sultan Khan, and he was an American.[2]

Powell's point vis-à-vis my thesis is that religion and society are interdependent cultural phenomenon. If religion is injected into the discourse of the public square, it should, as Jürgen Habermas has contended, be given in accord with the democratic values of truth, justice, and human dignity, and not accorded special privilege.[3]

An assumption of this study is that culture and theology are, and ought to be, intertwining and correlated phenomenon—they influence and are influenced by each other. In the categories of H. Richard Niebuhr outlined in *Christ and Culture* (Alumni Foundation Lecture at Austin Presbyterian Theological Seminary, 1949), though the variables may be in opposition—synthesis or paradoxical synergy—among other interactions, they inevitably shape and are shaped by each other.[4] Theology can influence secular society for good or for ill. Social reality can companion faith too much or too little. The world can be "too much with us" or we can miss Bonhoeffer's call for faith at the center of our "worldly existence."

The election season of 2008 revealed the beauty and ugliness of these interacting dimensions in the common life we now experience as nations and global society. Is American hegemony overseas a good mission in the world or at least a necessity of our security or, is it an unconscionable violation of the sovereignty of other nations and exploitation of their re-

2. Colin Powell, interview with Tom Brokaw, *Meet the Press*, NBC, October 19, 2008.

3. See Habermas, "Religion in the Public Sphere," also see Ratzinger and Habermas, *Dialectic of Secularization*.

4. See H. Richard Niebuhr, *Christ and Culture* and Part Three of this volume, 69–71.

sources? Is the economic crisis about greed, exploitation of the vulnerable poor, deception and a philosophical/theological corruption of capitalism, or is it about inevitable natural cycles and therefore a corroboration of the natural laws of economics (*e.g.*, Adam Smith, *laissez-faire* economics)?[5] On the energy front, are we undertaking responsibility and good stewardship on earth or are we reprehensibly degrading and destroying the goodness of God's creation?

THESIS

The thesis I am putting forward grounds norms for public action in a biblical-theological heritage. My particular take on this tradition is mediated through the Reformed Christian tradition, corroborated by the wider universal Christian tradition (Roman Catholic and Orthodox) as well as the beliefs and behavioral values of Judaism and Islam. This theological worldview is characterized by prophetic and progressive dimensions. On the one hand, it critiques extant policies where they miss the marks of divine will and inter-human justice. The constructive side of the ethic works to create concrete policies that honor God, edify human goods, and seek the imperatives of peace with justice.

From this perspective, *America in God's World* explores three sociocultural realms—security, economy, and ecology—across four process dimensions:

1. the crisis objectively outlined;

2. the constitutive wrong-doing;

3. a normative biblical position; and

4. a proposed theological correction and resolution.

Security

In exploring America's place in God's world, we consider initially the realm of militarism and might—policies to insure national safety at home and vested interests abroad (*e.g.*, energy to run the nation's engine). As people of God, we are to be advocates of all national sovereignties in a

---

5. *Laissez-faire* philosophy, popular in the late nineteenth and twentieth centuries, suggests that capitalism is most effective without government intervention. Adam Smith was instrumental in articulating *laissez-faire* economic policies in English-speaking countries. For a discussion of Adam Smith's economic concepts, see Part Two, 50–51.

world that we share as a commonwealth. God "has made of one blood all nations to dwell on the face of the earth, determining the times and bounds of their habitations" (Acts 17:26). We are the advocates of nation Israel and nation Iran, even though certain exigencies may make us temporarily adversaries. National and global security are therefore mandates. Homeland security in a safe, respectful, and peaceful world is the right of all nations. In addition to defense of motherland, this means protection from attack, invasion, and occupation. Security, then, is the first thematic topic explored in all four sections of this book.

Economy

Economy is the second cross-cutting theme. Resources, work, commerce, trade, and livelihood are perquisites of the well-being of all peoples in God's world—including America. Theologically conceived, work is the blessing and curse of existence. It is the task that both animates and ages our being, bestowing joy and drudgery. Writ large, economy is the management and stewardship of the local, national and global house—*oikos*—the habitation and cohabitation of our space/time being in the world. Economy, a cultural phenomenon with deep theological resonance, is proffered providence and the sphere of justice and sharing. Now it has become secular in meaning to the danger point of losing its ethical and theological charter.

For good and ill, economy is the enclosing envelope of our co-humanity—inciting both virtue and violence. Crisis has ensued as *ora et labora* has become tedious, hand labor has been converted to industry, then business, then management, and finally into abstract systems such as finance. Do such virtual powers exist? Virtually, yes. Should they?—a legitimate question. This fall from face-to-face and hand-to-hand dealings to "virtual finance" is highly problematic. "Finance," a new entity created by entrepreneurs seeking profits and fees, is made up of an array of phenomena called hedge funds, leverage, securitization, and bundled liquid assets. It is, in large, a human fabrication in the past few years, perhaps a demonic structure in the biblical language of "the powers of the world."

In the fallen world, these exist over against the power of God.[6] This unjust and inhuman system of virtual transactions culminates in the sad spectacle of no one in the world knowing who owns my mortgage. We

---

6. See Wink, *The Powers That Be, Engaging the Powers, Naming the Powers* and *Unmasking the Powers*; and Migliore, *Power of God.*

also see it when General Motors Corporation pleads for financial bailout from the only still viable financial entity—the federal government—that pale facsimile of the sacred body politic. Economics rightly belongs to *ecumene*—the one God-derived habitation for all humanity—so it must not become a demonic human construal bringing injury and death to humanity and the world itself.

Ecology

Environment is the third parameter at play across our analytical matrix. If our aggression abroad and repression of danger at home overtax resources, then the carrying capacity of the environment can turn against us. Security ultimately ends in circling the wagons, still-life, frozen section, and mortality. If our exploitation and appropriation of the given economic stores turns into printing baseless money and mortgaging our children—as in post-Versailles Germany or Mugabe's Africa—then economy turns empty or frozen. Ecology is a realm of inherent boundaries or quarantines. There is no free lunch and no infinite expansion. Malignant growth is eventually encapsulated or silenced by necrosis. Death is the ultimate constraint on unbridled growth. Mortgagers, credit card maxed-outers, and deficit-crazed nations are always moving from one depletion to the next until they repent, find *metanoia*, and renew their corporeal vitality or go bankrupt and die.

Part One offers an empirical evaluation of this tri-dimensional crisis in which America finds itself in these early years of the twenty-first century. Part Two begins the normative task of finding out what has gone wrong. Part Three adds creative proposals to the critical prophesies by showing pathways of correction and renewal. These pathways then suggest a summary formulation for America in God's World in Part Four. From a descriptive setting forth of the issues facing America and the world at the dawn of the twenty-first century, the argument moves through normative positions—critical and constructive—finally concluding with suggestive directions for the future.

1

Crisis in the Land

SECURITY

Bases Around the World

Thirst for Global Military Power

THE FIRST CRISIS THAT shakes the world is a disruption of the plan for divine and human justice given in the biblical witness and in corroborative human wisdom (*e.g.*, Kant's *Perpetual Peace*[1]). Contributing to this crisis is America's tendency to seek imperial power over the world by extending military hegemony, economic supremacy, and political domination in the service of its inappropriate and non-viable consumptive society. These actions usurp resources from others in the world and require political and economic servitude to satisfy our thirst for power.

This global ambition is animated by an underlying theology that itself diverges from the biblical mandates of how we are to live in God's world. The purpose of this section is to describe America's extant and dangerous program of domination in the world—with an eye toward correcting not only the underlying theology but also the policies and programs that flow from that worldview. The persuasion I offer in support of this argument is articulated by Barack Obama, in his courageous claim that our greatness in the world does not lie in our military might but rather in our finest ideals. "Not by might, but by my spirit, says the Lord" (Zech 4.6).

A window into this imperial program can be seen in the disengagement/security pact now being negotiated between the United States and

---

1. In his 1795 essay, "Perpetual Peace: A Philosophical Sketch," Kant outlines the requirements for achieving peace, (which he considers to be inevitable), including individual freedom, republican government, and a league of nations.

the Iraqi government. When can (must) the coalition troops be withdrawn? What off-site bases will be allowed in the long haul? Must the U.S. agree not to attack (invade and occupy) other nations from such bases? At this time in history, we may question Toynbee's designation of America as the most recent in the line of 18 world empires. His index of characteristics of existing and waning empires is highly controversial.[2] Within the malaise and ambiguity of the present "war on terrorism" and the global economic crisis, it appears that America is more a "reluctant empire" than a triumphalist and dominating force.

Despite its decreasing influence, however, America remains the dominant military and economic power in the world. The U.S. military budget is equal to that of the next 20 nations combined. The breadth and strength of our military primacy is established by the network of land-based, sea-based, and air-born installations of military power throughout the world. This visible presence is augmented by a surveillance apparatus of homeland and global security undertaken by an advanced technology and a highly sophisticated human network active around the world.

In addition to the presence the U.S. established after the great world wars in Europe and the Cold War (Europe, Japan, Korea), a more ubiquitous presence is continually being sought now in the Middle East, Eastern Europe, Africa, and Asia. This recent incursion into the Middle East and the regions of Islam is particularly aggravating to that community, becoming the precipitating cause of the events of September 11th and the war on terrorism.

In fact, the U.S. now has 700 military bases in 130 countries. This global array of high-tech intelligence and troop deployability is backed by an air and ocean presence instantly available for support and by a formidable "air mobility command" at each base. In addition to the historic post-war establishments (Asia and Europe), we find an impressive array of bases in "the new Europe"—Romania and Poland, as well as Pakistan, India, Morocco, Senegal, Mali, and so forth. The Persian Gulf contingent of bases is especially impressive because of the strategic importance of the region by virtue of oil and geopolitical concerns. This locus is also the homeland of the monotheistic faiths.

The cornerstone of this global edifice is a policy with clear theological and political underpinnings. Evolving from Wilsonian (WWI) assertion,

2. See Toynbee, *A Study of History*.

to conciliation, to WWII resistance against fascism and Marshall-Plan reconciliation and reconstruction of Europe and Asia, to Cold War/hot war (Korea and Viet Nam) Détente and collapse of communism, the U.S. has at last achieved its ambition of being the world's single super-power—befitting its theological identity and aspirations.

RESPONSES TO U.S. POLICY AND LEADERSHIP

New features of the policy guiding America's global role include the desire to purvey liberty and democracy throughout the world's regions and peoples. A missionary zeal and articulation betrays an implicit (and often explicit) theological sense of destiny that we will subsequently see as both glorious and dangerous. At present, the glory often becomes boasting triumphalism on our part, engendering resentment and resistance (as often as hope and thanksgiving) on the recipient's part. Cold-War and post-Cold-War endeavors in Asia, Africa, and the Americas often have been rejected as neo-colonial and neo-conservative abuse.

In 2007, the Pew Global Attitudes Project revealed that "global distrust of American leadership is reflected in increasing disapproval of the cornerstones of U.S. foreign policy. Not only is there worldwide support for a withdrawal of U.S. troops from Iraq, but also there is considerable opposition to U.S. and NATO operations in Afghanistan. Western European publics are at best divided about keeping troops there. In nearly every predominantly Muslim country, overwhelming majorities want U.S. and NATO troops withdrawn from Afghanistan as soon as possible. In addition, global support for the U.S.-led war on terrorism ebbs, and the United States is the nation blamed most often for hurting the world's environment, at a time of rising global concern about environmental issues."[3]

Certain ideas in the articulation of America's place in the world have become especially problematic in recent decades. Today, as Jimmy Carter, Nelson Mandela, and Kofi Annan attempt to enter Zimbabwe hoping to effect reconciliation, they are turned back at the border because of the residue of suspicion and fear regarding America's duplicitous motives. Recent policies—including "preemptive strikes," invasion and occupation actions, unilateralism, and blatant hypocrisy—often have turned the world against us. Claiming to be advocates of justice and peace in the world while rejecting the Kyoto Climate Change Treaty, withdrawing

3. The Pew Global Attitudes Project, "Global Unease With Major World Powers," Pew Research Center, http://pewglobal.org/reports/pdf/256.pdf.

from the International Criminal Court, and canceling the bio-weapons and ABM (anti-ballistic missile) nuclear accords—these actions have not served us well. The "Bush Doctrine" of counter-terrorism, especially in its aspects of torture, suspending human rights, and resisting national sovereignties, has caused a significant shift in the world's perception of the U.S. Especially striking is one aspect of the country's changing attitude toward human rights: as Conor Gearty points out in *Can Human Rights Survive?*, "the unspeakable is no longer unspoken . . . Even the greatest of our human rights taboos—the prohibition on torture and inhuman and degrading treatment—has become just another point of view . . ."[4] These policies, actions, and attitudes have caused the U.S. to be perceived more as a force *against* rather than *for* freedom, justice, and peace in the world.

American Exceptionalism

THE FALLACY OF EXCEPTIONALISM

If a theological error lies at the root of this disorientation toward the world community, it may be found in what is called American exceptionalism. Even if vice-presidential candidate Sarah Palin brought some dishonor to the phrase, it remains a resonant theme in the religious and political life of this nation. Though necessary, the process of deconstructing and reconstructing our popular theology about this ambition will prove difficult for two reasons. Empirically speaking, between the collapse of the Russian empire and the rising of the Chinese, we are *de facto* the singular superpower in the world. We may be forced, as world Jewry often has found necessary, to disclaim the designation as the "chosen people." "Please God," we also might cry, "choose someone else!" In this vein, there might even be a residual truth in the assertion that, if we could creatively transpose the biblical dictum, "to whom much is given, much will be required" (Luke 12.48). But this, too, may be a burden too heavy to be borne.

Secondly, the theology seems to make common sense. In the election of 2008 in America, both Barack Obama and John McCain espoused an understanding of the nation as exceptional. Obama asked the rhetorical question, "In what other nation in the world would it be possible for one such polyglot and international person" (a white mother and African father/raised in Indonesia/with the name 'Barack') "to rise to be the

---

4. Gearty, *Can Human Rights Survive?*, 132.

President of the United States of America?" He often concluded his stump speeches with the words, "we are not red states and blue states... we are the United States of America...Black, White, Asian, Hispanic, male, female, gay, straight, rich, poor ... God bless you and God bless America...the last best hope in the world." Patriotism and nationalism are part of the warp and woof of the political ethos and the popular religion. In actuality, these assertions are absurd and idiosyncratic. Obama might well have excelled wherever he grew up. At variance with our exceptionalist and xenophobic customs, exceptionalism in scripture pertains to all nations:

> God has made of one blood all nations, determining the times and bounds of their habitation, that they should seek the Lord and find Him ... (Acts 17.26).

ORIGINS OF AMERICAN EXCEPTIONALISM

American exceptionalism has a fascinating and controversial history. We Americans often have worn the badge with pride. Think of the joy greeting our liberating troops in the German cities of Hitler's waning *Dritte Reich*—quite in contrast to the reception we received in Viet Nam and Iraq. Exceptionalism also has been a disputed and unwelcome doctrine to Native, African, and Hispanic Americans. A mixed-bag of component virtues and values is designated by the phrase. It can refer to liberty, equality, and democracy. But it also connotes the more complex values of individualism, populism, and non-interference (*laissez-faire*).

Theologically, the idea becomes even more complex and, on the one hand, relates to the Puritan notions of religious chosenness and "City on a Hill"—the celestial beacon of liberty and equality for the whole world to see—not to be "hid under the bushel" (Matt 5–7). Walking the tightrope between strict Calvinists, with their doctrine of divine providence that left no room for boasting, and a more Arminian (Dutch and Methodist) confidence in human works and achievement, the religious component of exceptionalism highlighted the doctrine of *cooperatio dei*—a divine destiny achieved by siding and collaborating with the warrior God—the justice-avenger, righteousness-achiever, and peace-maker.

On the other hand, religious authorization of American exceptionalism flows in part from Deism and the wall of separation between church and state. Here, liberation and kingdom-of-God theology (*e.g.*, Rauschenbusch[5])

5. See Rauschenbusch, *Christianity and the Social Crisis.*

takes on a character much in the spirit of secular enlightenment. Thomas Paine's "Common Sense"—still the hermeneutical principle of biblical interpretation of Yale University, a colonial establishment—and Abraham Lincoln's sublime vision of "Liberty, (Equality) and Justice for all" resonate with this theological impulse.

Critical Analysis of American Exceptionalism

In an interview with recently deceased Nobel Literature Laureate Harold Pinter, Charlie Rose raised the issue of American exceptionalism. Here is my summary and paraphrase:[6]

> CR: From your writing and speaking, it appears that you believe there is something about the U.S., something at the core of its being, history, and destiny, which evokes terror and violence throughout the world, especially the Islamic world.
>
> HP: Yes, there is something about the U.S. that terrifies the world and makes possible disgraces like Guantanamo and *Abu Ghraib.*
>
> CR: What we do is not what we are!
>
> HP: Persons like Bush, Blair, Cheney, and Rumsfeld should be tried for war crimes.

Augmenting this perspective is that of Andrew Bacevich, a historian of military power and International Relations—a student of Reinhold Niebuhr. In his new study, *The Limits of Power: The End of American Exceptionalism,*[7] he locates his perspective as a "realist" in the Niebuhrian tradition. A Catholic and conservative in sketching his critical philosophical persuasion, Bacevich argues that the "arrogant and narcissistic" politics of the U.S. "have brought the country to the brink of interlocking crises: economic (cultural), political, and military."[8] Bacevich supports, in part, my thesis that the root crisis is a spiritual and moral malaise. A retired colonel from the U.S. Army, he finds causal concerns in our materialism and an inappropriate militarism that is erroneously fueled by the heresy of American exceptionalism.

---

6. Harold Pinter, interview with Charlie Rose, *The Charlie Rose Show*, PBS, March 1, 2007.

7. See Bacevich, *The Limits of Power.*

8. Michiko Kakutani, "A Dialogue and Discourse on America's Global Role," *The New York Times*, September 23, 2008, B7.

Economic and Cultural

Bacevich first cites materialism—the "shop until you drop" syndrome—as symptomatic of American economic profligacy grounded in the deluded blessedness and invulnerability of exceptionalism, rather than the lack of gratitude and commensurate anxiety that actually animate the shopping spree and materialistic impulse. This characteristic is the precursor of "maxed-out" credit cards and bad mortgage paper—core injustices in the present U.S.-led global economic crisis. The tragic perfect storm we now experience is the conjunction of what political-theological critic Ivan Illich calls ravenous consumers and rapacious providers.

Bacevich suggests that a "becoming" and "good" exceptionalism might well be grounded in the causes of truth, justice, freedom that we will live and die for in this world of anguish and strife, and based in the heart of love to the poor, sick, aged, homeless, refugees, and immigrants—the wretched of the world who have been drawn to these shores and invade our consciousness and conscience through global communications. Such values also are a constituting constellation of virtue in the founding heritage of this nation.

Political

Bacevich then draws the mischievous—not salutary—connection between abundance and power. Inextricably intertwined, as we see more and more each day, are globalization, economics, foreign policy, and international intervention. Former Secretary of State James Baker once candidly remarked that if Iraq's prime export was oranges instead of oil—there would be no war.

Time-Life publisher Henry Luce, who after 1945, felt that a special destiny was bestowed on America given its sacrificial leadership in challenging the force of European and Asian fascism, proposed this new place in the world with all the zeal that a son of missionaries could muster. In his claims about the American Century, Luce used the language of exceptionalism to describe the U.S. as the strongest, richest, and most free nation in the world, a manifest destiny, the blessing of an Invisible Hand, a city on a hill with limitless hope and blessing. Captain America was set to rule the world.

The sentiment is seconded and given theological substance in a new book by Zbigniew Brzezinski and Brent Scowcroft—two seasoned veterans of American foreign policy, one liberal and one conservative and both savvy in international understanding and ethics.

Political realists cut from Niebuhrian cloth, they allude to Niebuhr's Gifford Lectures of 1937 on "The Nature and Destiny of Man": "The more a civilization approaches its downturn, the more fervently it proclaims its supremacy. There's a warning in that. We have tended, in recent years, to define world affairs in Manichaean[9] terms. We are the epitome of right. Those who are not with us are against us. Those who are against us are by definition evil. I think we ought to be a little more modest about our place in the world."[10] And so my thesis.

Military

In a personal and deeply moving tribute on the front cover of *The Limits of Power*, Bacevich dedicates the book to his son with these words: "To the memory of my beloved son," (an astute theologian, Bacevich may allude here to Gen 22 and John 3.16) "Andrew John Bacevich, First Lieutenant, U.S. Army (July 8, 1979—May 13, 2007)." Then, he adds from 2 Kings 20.1, "Set thine house in order."

In his discussion of military crises, Bacevich laments the half century of international misadventures and military mistakes following the nobility of our early-century resistance to the imperial tyranny of Germany, Japan, and subsequently, Russia. These misadventures included—to his mind—Korea, Viet Nam, and most recently Iraq, and the terribly complicated war on international terrorism.

Rather than sorting through the tangled questions of the legitimacy of twentieth-century wars, Bacevich seeks a theological hermeneutic of understanding grounded in Reinhold Niebuhr. He first recalls how Niebuhr warns against misusing our excellent gift of foundational freedom. This Puritan construal of the destiny and calling of nations in the divine economy, where justice and peace are seen as the concomitants of righteousness and constituitive freedom, leaves no room for arrogance

9. Manichaeism, a religion dating back to a Persian named Mani in the third century CE, is characterized by a belief in a conflicting dualism between God, symbolized by light and Spirit, and Satan, represented by darkness and matter.

10. Brzezinski and Scowcroft, *America and the World*, 268. Similarly, Oswald Spengler argues that all cultures experience a life cycle made up of repeating patterns of rise and falls. For more on his theories, see Spengler, et al., *The Decline of the West*. See also Toynbee, *A Study of History*, for his index of characteristics of existing and waning empires.

and narcissism. "Restless and striving," wrote Niebuhr, "the American people seek a solution for the practical problems of life in quantitative terms."[11] Long before Lucy in Charles Schultz's "Peanuts," we Americans became a collective body that wanted "only ups and ups and ups."[12]

In addition to this restless striving, materialism and a reluctance to incorporate limits and the rightful claims of the needy into economic philosophies and practices have set the world on edge. Max Weber remarked after he and Ernst Troeltsch appeared at the 1904 World's Fair in St. Louis that America's economic thirst for prosperity in the here and hereafter would infect the rest of the world. This infection not only carried the germs of freedom, democracy, free markets, and free enterprise, but also of competitor-eliminating competition, greed, lethal envy, enormous disparity of rich and poor, and terminal anxiety. Now Europe, China, Africa, even India and Asia have caught the flu.

Bacevich concludes his critique of the American sociocultural psyche—that gives rise to such bizarre and contradictory impulses in the realms of economy, polity, and military—by citing Niebuhr's concern that we now cling to beliefs and values that make "standards of living" the final norm of the good life and the "perfection of technique" as the guarantor of every cultural as well as every social-moral value.[13] In Neibuhr's great masterpiece, *The Nature and Destiny of Man,* he views it as a rudimentary anthropological heresy to make instrumental intelligence and technical virtuosity the end and meaning of life. The trait and act become the deep stain of our collective intelligence sullying personal and public life. A "can-do" and "can-fix" mentality becomes the foundation of a false security whose ultimate fallacy is "the security of power." The primal temptation has thus become the temptation of nations and empires.[14]

In its modern transmutation, American exceptionalism becomes the proverbial "American Dream" and our "way of life." Recent opposition to tyranny becomes the leitmotif of American exceptionalism, as historical consciousness is influenced by the two world wars against fascist tyranny and Cold-War resistance to collectivism.

11. Reinhold Niebuhr, *The Irony of American History,* 3, 56, 92.

12. M. Thomas Inge, *Charles M. Schultz: Conversations* (Jackson: University Press of Mississippi, 2004), 24.

13. Reinhold Niebuhr, *The Irony of American History,* 57.

14. Reinhold Niebuhr, *The Nature and Destiny of Man* and *Beyond Tragedy,* 98.

This survey of a salient idea bears out G.K. Chesterton's judgment that ". . . America is the only nation in the world founded on a creed. The creed is set forth with dogmatic and even theological lucidity in the Declaration of Independence."[15]

For most of the time, American exceptionalism is a pejorative. Any "divine-calling" theology of the nation becomes especially irksome to a world in which our prestige has suffered so badly. America's origins, by contrast, are found in revolution and enlightenment (both secular and religious). The Great Awakening—associated with the names of Edwards, Wesley, and Whitfield—shows the more commendable and exemplary dimensions of the American exceptionalism designation—in the sense of divine responsibility, renewal of the world (cf. John Milton), edification and justice for the poor, and a missionary zeal for and proffered humility among the peoples of the world.

The Bush Agenda

CENTRAL TENETS OF THE BUSH DOCTRINE

Governor Sarah Palin wasn't quite sure what it was when queried by a news correspondent. It turns out there are several senses of the term— the Bush Doctrine—which should not be a surprise to such an icon of "Saturday Night Live." Does it refer to the doctrine formulated some 20 years ago around the University of Chicago on American global strategy over signatures such as Paul Wolfowitz, Richard Perle, Douglas Feith, and Dick Cheney? Does it refer to the post-September 11th doctrine formulated in the White House as our national response to terrorists— whose attacks on American interests began decades ago and reached a cruel and grotesque apex in the flaming and crumbling twin towers of the World Trade Center?

The cardinal document seems to be a Bush speech given at West Point in 2002.[16] The doctrine has been refined on a regular basis over time, as events would dictate, leading to a position on troop withdrawal in Iraq very much like the Obama doctrine of recent months. The two leitmotifs of the doctrine are the "war on terrorism" and the "democracy

---

15. Chesterton, *The Collected Works of G.K. Chesterton*, 41.

16. George W. Bush, Graduation Address, June 1, 2002, U.S. Military Academy, West Point, New York.

agenda." The *Economist* has identified five key elements that elaborate the central tenets of the Bush Doctrine:

- America is at war with global terrorism and must respond to state sponsors of terrorism.

- Preemptive attack is the best form of defense to prevent threats from materializing.

- To preserve freedom to act independently, America should not "lock in" with global bodies that may act too slowly.

- Use global power to encourage allies and dissuade enemies.

- Export democracy as the best antidote to *Jihadism*.[17]

FORCES OF CHANGE

The lingering malaise in Iraq and the U.S. role as the *avant garde*, if not the precipitating cause of the global economic crisis, has wounded our sense of virtue—tainting global deliverance with lies and torture and benevolence with greed and dishonesty. The election showed that the simplistic carica-ture of Islam as a monolithic radical-terrorist entity simply does not pass muster even with neo-conservatives, the military, and bar-stool patriots.

While the Bush Doctrine may lie in ruins, some elements will need to be retained. American confidence should be reawakened in the Obama administration, and that confidence should be repositioned in our justice, generosity, good will, mutuality, care for the earth, and provision for the poor. Such policy will make it easier to out-influence global *Jihad*—if such a cohesive movement actually does exist.

Interfaith dialogue, which is dramatically rising around the world, holds great promise. Exemplified by documents developed in all sectors of Christendom and those bookended by our Semitic siblings—"*Dabru Emet*" in Judaism and "A Common Word" in Islam—the religious world is poised to bring about huge strides in international religious understand-ing.[18] As violent religious fanaticism—*al Qaeda*, for example—seems to

17. "America and the World: Can the Bush Doctrine Last," *The Economist*, May 27, 2008, www.economist.com/surveys/displaystory.cfm?story_id=10873479.

18. "*Dabru Emet*" is a Jewish statement that articulates eight principles to guide Jewish-Christian relations; for more information, see the Jewish-Christian Relations Web site, www.jcrelations.net/en/?item=1014. "A Common Word," the work of Muslim scholars, clerics, and intellectuals, identifies the common ground between Islam and Christianity. The complete document is available on the Web site of A Common Word, www.acommonword.com/.

be losing credibility and popular support throughout the world, perhaps a new irenic interfaith consciousness may be taking hold.

ECONOMY

Bad Money

A FAILING ECONOMY

> ... Economics is the greatest challenge facing this country (and the world) in our generation, since the great depression, in the last 100 years ...[19]

"The patient has atherosclerosis—vessel blockage. He is on the verge of heart-attack." No alarmist, Princeton Professor and Fed Chairman Ben Bernanke went on with the deft scalpel of a heart surgeon, suggesting that $1 trillion now invested in revascularization and a stent might spare us a myocardial infarction—the heart attack to come.[20] What the doctor failed to mention was that Bush/Greenspan deregulation (lack of preventive medicine) allowed "fast-buck seekers" to take on $40 trillion in debt with only $1 trillion in the bank—hypertension and plaque build-up, to say the least, and an exhausting deflation of the balloon to come. As of Thanksgiving 2008, the American people had lost $12 trillion in wealth and assets—$5 trillion in housing values and $7 trillion in the stock market. "Moral hazard" already has set in, wherein financiers take risks because of support forthcoming from taxpayers exposing themselves to acute breakdown. We need "jolt" and jar—stability and security. We're in the ICU.

Congress had been asked by Treasury Secretary Hank Paulson to approve a massive infusion of funds to absorb "toxic debts"(primarily predatory mortgages) held by Freddie Mac, Fannie Mae, Bear Stearns, AIG, and other companies—and thus relieve the "financial structure." The financial structure is an entity that has evolved in recent years, a kind of epiphenomenon built on the ageless foundations of barter, business, and commerce previously called "the economy." Economic historian Kevin

19. At a Chicago news conference on November 7, 2008, Barack Obama said "We are facing the greatest economic challenge of our lifetime...," and in subsequent speeches, he reiterated the serious economic hurdles facing the U.S.

20. Chris Isidore, "Hopes Grow for Emergency Rate Cut," *CNN Money*, September 26, 2008, http://money.cnn.com.

Phillips warned that this new elephant in the room—created in the main to satisfy the enormous thirst among bankers and brokers for intensifying and accelerating fees and profits—posed an ominous threat to the nation and world:

> . . . far more worrisome than the problem (debt and oil-related economic transformations of the last two or three decades) is the possibility that neither Washington nor Wall Street is willing to confront the deeper problem—the ascendancy of finance in national policymaking . . . and the complicity of politicians who really don't want to talk about it.[21]

As I write, the world remains in economic shock. It began about six weeks ago when the financial crisis announced by Fed Chairman Bernanke and Treasury Secretary Paulson was amplified into the crisis of the general and global economy—corporation profits, unemployment statistics, and stock market values. The shock played some part in Obama's landslide election. Since that time, European banks have made dramatic cuts in their interest rates—Germany, one point and England, one-and-a-half points.

Economic Bubbles and Greed

Idolatry, Immorality, and Injustice

Economic behaviors have been influenced by misguided religious convictions—such as those of the so-virtuous Enron executives—that have led to unethical imperatives: rebellious and ungracious religiously animated greed, presumption of righteousness (idolatry), injustice, and contempt for the poor—all on a grand scale. This combination of corporate vice and the consumptive consumers behind it constitutes the evil at the root of the economic crisis.

> . . . they that will be rich fall into temptation and a snare...For the love of money is the root of all evil: which while some coveted after, they have erred from the faith and pierced themselves through with many sorrows" (I Tim 6.9–10).

In salient theological/ethical insight, Judaic conviction at the time of Jesus (*e.g.*, Qumran) perceived evil ("the snares of Belial"/the devil) as

---

21. Phillips, *Bad Money*, vii.

threefold: blasphemy (false gods/idolatry), *Porneia* (false loves/immorality), and riches (false possessions/injustice).

What happened in the inner meaning of reality—what, after Karen Armstrong, I will call "the history of God"—is that the diminishing sector of humanity, those who "own" and control the lion's share of the world's wealth, have seen their "riches" turn against them. That one percent of the human family has intensified their theft from the poor (ignoring the eighth commandment: "Do not steal") and has seen the "strong arm of justice" turn against them.

> Truth forever on the scaffold, Wrong forever on the throne,
> Yet that scaffold sways the future, and, behind the dim unknown,
> Standeth God within the shadow, keeping watch above his own.[22]

CONTRIBUTIONS OF THEOLOGY TO ECONOMICS

The crisis of economy in its religious and ethical dimensions was first outlined by Max Weber in his book, *The Protestant Ethic and the Spirit of Capitalism*.[23] The philosopher/economist reflected on the changes in economic attitudes and values in the rural and newly urban Rhineland conveyed by the wake of the nascent Protestant Reformation. His research showed the connection of political and economic history and the history of God. Quite rapidly, the Rhineland peasants were being dispossessed of their meager holdings on the land and being forced to foreclose and migrate to the destitution of urban centers as landholding development companies joined "house to house."

> He looked for justice but found oppression; for righteousness but heard a cry. Woe unto them who join house to house, that lay field to field, till there be no place that they may be placed in the midst of the earth. (Isa 5.7–8).

The underlying theological premise of these economic changes was the mischievous double notion that God prospers the righteous and that poverty discloses moral laxity. Weber traced two developments: peasant displacement and migration and the emergence of capitalism, banking, investment, and business—all within the framework of this religiosity. A descriptive sociologist, Weber refrained from condemnation or commen-

---

22. Russell, "The Present Crisis," 1844.
23. See Weber, *The Protestant Ethic*.

dation of these developments. While he noted the economic convictions of Luther's quietism, Calvin's transformationism, and Wesley's distributionism ("earn all you can, save all you can, give all you can"), he remained content to merely describe the processes of commercial management and labor and political legitimatization and implementation. Theology contributes to both the substance and process of economics.

Weber argues that the substance and structures of these economic processes were animated by religious beliefs within American Puritanism—Calvinism and Wesleyanism—beliefs such as chosenness and blessedness. In this society—which Weber called the epitome of capitalism in the world when he visited the St. Louis World's Fair in 1904—the poor also were to be dispossessed from a base on the land. While management in the Presbyterian and Methodist churches celebrated their prosperity, poor struggling laborers and layoffs were dealing in their storefronts with the insult added to injury of knowing they were perceived as spiritually laggard. In the 2008 election, a shift to Democratic (derisively called "socialist") values was seen throughout the country except, as one news outlet put it, "around the edge of the Appalachian mountains." Kevin Phillips comments on the economic crisis and the fact that nations around the world blame America—"Aren't we the good guys? people asked at Rotary lunches in Indianapolis and church picnics in Nashville."[24]

As this argument unfolds, it will become clear that the charge against Puritans, Calvinists, and Methodists holds up only as dispensationalism, a mid-nineteenth-century aberrational theology and Gnostic/Manichaean heresy,[25] a perennial temptation, takes hold within these otherwise salutary faith communities. The rapture, "left-behind" and end-times eschatology, America and Israel as "chosen" peoples, and American exceptionalism are foreign notions to Puritan, Calvinist, and Methodist movements as well as to the broad orthodox tradition of Christianity. The presumption

24. Phillips, *Bad Money*, 19.

25. Dispensationalism is a system of theology built on two orthodox doctrines—the incarnation and the return of Christ—and a vision of history occurring in different "dispensations," periods of time in which humans' obedience to God's will is tested. The father of modern dispensationalism is considered to be John Nelson Darby, a nineteenth-century Brethren minister who put forth the idea of a future restoration of Israel as part of the Old Testament promise. Current expressions of dispensationalism can be found among some American evangelicals and have entered the popular culture through the "Left-Behind" fiction series and a series of books by Hal Lindsey (*The Late Great Planet Earth* and others) featuring end-times scenarios and apocalyptic battles between good and evil.

of being the chosen, "in-the-know" few among the unenlightened many, and the tendency to project evil onto certain others (*e.g.*, Muslims, Jews, homosexuals) certainly are religious factors contributing to the crisis. The imperatives of truth, social justice, and peace embedded in the normative heritage from which these aberrations sway are essential to any resolution of the global crisis.

Kevin Phillips has prophetically studied my three intertwining parameters of security, economy, and ecology in their theological context through a series of books beginning with *The Cousins' Wars*, in which he explores the salutary and deleterious effects of American political Calvinism as it focused in the Piedmont and Appalachian regions.[26] This theology always has intrigued me, since it was the faith of my parents and grandparents on both sides and of the first Presbyterian churches I served as minister and the seminary at which I now teach. Pittsburgh Presbyterians, West Virginia Baptists, and Indiana Methodists—and the religio-political ethos they represent—formed an influential movement during the years of my ministry as pastor, teaching theologian, and ethics-consultant to public institutions. Issues of such religious influence and conflict arose during the terms of Eisenhower, LBJ, Jimmy Carter, and Bill Clinton, and during the McCain/Obama contest of 2008.

Phillips continued with a study called *American Theocracy: The Perils and Politics of Radical Religion, Oil and Borrowed Money in the 21st Century*, in which he explores the ethical culpability arising from an underlying deficient theology.[27] In his view, the "Christian Right" teaching that held sway during the eight years of the Bush/Cheney administration coincided with the rise of Muslim animosity toward the U.S. This animosity thwarted our aspirations toward Empire, forcing us into economy-spoiling deficit spending as Osama bin Laden continued his assaults on our military, economic, and political domains—beginning with the September 11th attacks on the Pentagon, Wall Street, and the White House. Gasoline prices, war expenditures, and furious greed-based profiteering in the financial sector finally burst the economic bubble and fulfilled bin Laden's malign dream of revenge.

26. See Phillips, *The Cousins' Wars*.
27. See Phillips, *American Theocracy*.

Turbulence in the Homeland

Once-lauded Fed Chairman Alan Greenspan, now chided for the *laissez-faire* posture that let mortgage lenders "run wild,"[28] has written a moving journal, *The Age of Turbulence*.[29] This history offers insight into the unfolding economic crisis. In an interview with Jim Lehrer, Greenspan likens the beginning ". . . of the bubble phenomenon in world markets" to "the epochal shift of rural workers to the cities in China."[30] He chronicles how the rural population of China peaked in 1995 at nearly 860 million. Eleven years later, in 2006, it was down to 737 million. The shift was not only the result of people moving to cities . . . but also the result of rural land being urbanized, as new manufacturing enclaves began to sprout up along the Pearl river delta contiguous to Hong Kong.[31] In other words, the transformation involved not only new opportunity, but also dispossession of the peasant poor from their inheritance and livelihood on the land. In the prophetic words of Ohio Congressman Dennis Kucinich, while we may see the human injustice in exploiting the poor, working people, the industrial and agrarian base, and people struggling to pay their mortgages—we are fattening the estates of the "financial" elite.

This dispossession of the poor, Greenspan claims, has led to greater inequality, a concentration of wealth, and the threat of inflation. He continues:

> I trace the roots of the most recent housing bubble and the stock market of the late 1990s to the remarkable sequence of events following the end of the Cold War: the nearly universal abandonment, the embrace of market economics, and the influx of half a billion people into the labor force of newly market-oriented economies across the globe.[32]

High-tech, Housing, Oil, and Finance Bubbles

The turbulence that Greenspan cites has led to boom-bust economics in the high-tech, housing, oil, and finance sectors—the peculiar mania of

28. Serwer and Sloan, "How Financial Madness Overtook Wall Street," *Time*, September 29, 2008.

29. See Greenspan, *The Age of Turbulence*.

30. Greenspan, interview with Jim Lehrer, *The NewsHour*, PBS, September 18, 2007.

31. Greenspan, *The Age of Turbulence*, 304.

32. Ibid., 510.

Anglo-American capitalism, according to Weber and his protégés for a century. It has sucked up wealth from workers and the poor so rapidly that this nation, which once was the leading lender nation in the world, is now its leading debtor.

> Around the world, in the years between 1985 and 2005, increases in the market value of stocks, bonds, residential and commercial real-estate, and home mortgages significantly outpaced the growth in global domestic income. These assets, when purchased by financial intermediaries, in turn generated a massive increase in liquidity. Investment banks, private equity funds, hedge funds, and pension funds were flushed with investible cash. Emboldened by signs of increasing stability, investors reached out to acquire lesser-grade, higher-yielding assets.[33]

Seeking the higher fees available from investment bundles and foreclosures, greed, and "fast-buck" impulses became the way of life for thousands of entrepreneurs. One banker involved in the sub-prime mortgage confessed in a television interview that the bank's bread-and-butter was made up of loans to the most vulnerable and most likely to foreclose—the disadvantaged, minorities and the poor. This calls to mind the famous Gospel picture of the Widow's mite: the Temple land-lawyers watched this poor widow with glee as she gave her last possession and now was doomed to repossession. In this view, Jesus' commendation may not only be for her generosity with little, but her blessedness in being "the persecuted for righteousness sake" (Mark 12.42, Luke 6.20).

Global Ripples

Sharing or Stealing

Theologically and ethically speaking, economy is a matter of sharing and/ or stealing. At present, we watch a spectacle on this matter in the seas off East Africa. Somalia pirates have commandeered hundreds of international ships and held their crews and cargo for ransom. Left without options, companies usually pay up. The U.S. and NATO cry to spend millions and send vast security and attack flotillas into the waters to break the barbarous and brazen acts of stealing. One wonders whether the outlay of funds might better be used to create jobs in the desperate economies

33. Ibid, 510.

of the horn of Africa. Do the pirates steal because we stole from them in the first place, *i.e.*, the colonial enterprise of extracting precious minerals (didn't the nativity gift of Frankincense originate in Mogadishu?) Sharing or stealing? Perhaps one prevents, provokes, or ameliorates the other.

POWER OF THE WORLD VS. POWER OF GOD

On November 17, 2008, *The New York Times* quoted a statement made in 2000 by Texas Republican Phil Gramm: "The work of this Congress will be seen as a watershed, where we turned away from the outmoded, Depression-era approach to financial regulation and adopted a framework that will position our financial-services industries to be world leaders into the new century."

A major architect of deregulation, former U.S. Senator Phil Gramm is one of the important founder-creators of the "financial-services industry." This novel entity, seemingly enjoying "hands-off autonomy"—even ontological status—has become Adam Smith's "Invisible Hand."[34] In truth, the verdict is not yet in whether the entity of "finance" is a salutary and necessary epiphenomenon of economic life in the world, an ethically ambiguous human construct, a "demonic power" sucking up the wealth from the poor and from workers of the world, or a "power of the world" set against the "power of God." Some say it is an artifact of our greed and injustice. Others say that "finance" is the lifeblood of our nation—worthy of first rescue. "Finance" may be as ethereal and vanishing as Bernard Madoff's billions. One commentator remarked that capital is our life-blood—and we are a capitalist nation (and perhaps world?). Salvation or damnation—the verdict is still out. Can societies endure and survive the "financial sector?" In Britain, one in five persons now works in this sector. In America, it is one in 18, and New York City receives 30 percent of its revenues from the financial sector. Could it be that societies have to create such "virtual entities" to put its people to work? Demographers now estimate that each physician carries 50 health-care workers in his or her path—perhaps a good thing for a service-based economy.

Finance may be a more mischievous fiction and fabrication. Former Commerce Secretary William Daley pipes the dream that may support

---

34. Adam Smith's concept of the Invisible Hand describes a process by which each individual attempts to profit for his or her own sake—through exchanging goods with others who values these offerings—and, in doing so, public interest is advanced. For more on this concept, see Part Two, pages 50–53.

30 percent of the lawyers in the Anglo-American world. "If the financial system breaks, the whole society goes down."[35] Obviously we are dealing with a multicolored Chicago "sacred cow" with not-so-pretty spots.

ECOLOGY

Black Gold

MAN VS. THE ENVIRONMENT

As I write on November 15, 2008, *Gehenna* fires sweep across Southern California. Thousands have been evacuated, and millions—suffering under 100 degree temperatures—are told not to use energy and power because supply lines from the East are threatened by the lashing flames and 75 mph Santa Ana winds. One wonders whether such natural disasters fall into pattern with the other crises I explore. Should people seek to inhabit geological faults, flood zones on the world's great waters, tinderbox forests on paradisal California mountains, or the Mississippi Delta in New Orleans exposed to the double jeopardy of Gulf hurricanes? Are crises "acts of God" or avoidable ethical actions of society? Economist Amartya Sen argues that poverty, even famines, involve human contrivance. Thoughtful social policies can predict, avoid, and otherwise ameliorate many calamities we chalk up to "acts of God."

Maintaining environmental sustainability—while meeting the voracious appetite for energy to fuel vibrant economies that lift the quality of life of the populace—has become the paramount concern of the U.S., which now imports 70 percent of its energy needs. Sustainability is now the surpassing concern in Asia, Europe, and the rest of the world. In the U.S., environment seems to be sliding onto the back-burner as jobs and health care—survival and well-being—become more prominent. Ecological responsibility regrettably is not seen as an urgent issue, a matter of life and death, as it surely would be if we had adequate predictive knowledge of the results of what we were now doing to the earth, water, skies, and the animal and human world.

---

35. William Daley, interview with Carol Marin, *Chicago Tonight*, WTTW, November 24, 2008.

BLACK GOLD

Oil is my first parameter. This natural substance and resource has provided energy for the world for 100-plus years. Augmenting the thousands of years of heat and power provided by wood, then peat, then coal, black gold became the occasion for human societies to reinvent themselves into cultures of industry, to warm modern homes even in frigid climes, to fuel high-speed transportation by rail, air, and road with what history will surely see as dinosaurs, but even more treacherous—vehicles fueled by internal-combustion engines.

Now we face a world populace of ravenous consumers and rapacious providers, each of its seven billion lives requiring in a lifetime a small section of forest, a good portion of a coal mine, a signature dot on a skyline dotted with nuclear plants, or a generous and regrettably terminal siphon on earth's vast reservoir of oil and natural gas. Using a modern idiom, we could say that each of us leaves an indelible carbon Bigfoot-print on the sands of time, and nature groans under the force of our presence.

Ecological Degradation

THE GOD-OIL CONNECTION

The most ominous footprint of the energy crisis is global warming—the melting of the polar ice caps and the meltdown of the globe's air conditioner and solar defense shield. We may be in for, it seems, not only persistent fires and floods and the extinction of beloved life-species such as polar bears and whales, but also human diseases—especially radiation-triggered malignancies such as melanoma and skin cancer.

Richard Cizik of the evangelical movement in America has come to the view that environment is a "sanctity-of-life" issue.[36] Close reading of the 2008 election returns shows that the evangelical community has moved in that direction. The glacial shift in religious sentiment has profound implications for America in our world. What might be called "evangelical theology" has enormous importance on the salutary and deleterious side of environmental issues, as well as all ethico-political issues. As I explore these issues, I seek to distinguish the theologies that are contributive and constructive from those that may be negating and destruc-

36. Richard Cizik, interview with National Public Radio, *Fresh Air*, NPR, December 2, 2008.

tive in helping us deal with concerns in which the world and life itself is at stake. Constructive theology is not blandly pietistic or syncretistic in interfaith awareness. It seeks truth and right as opposed to accommodation. Worldly reality and the reality of God are codependent and require reciprocal affirmation and critique.

Kevin Phillips best makes the God-oil connection. Oil has become for twentieth- and twenty-first-century America and the world what wind and water were for seventeenth-century Holland and what coal was for eighteenth- and nineteenth-century England. It is the staff and substance of life—black gold. Without oil—which now anchors the U.S. and world economy (a role previously consigned to the gold standard)—the lights would go out and movement would slow to a stand-still. Hospitals, houses of worship, schools, electronics, and the hum of life itself would grow silent. God, we fear—who is vitality, life, and *exousia* (power)—might fall away. Without oil, we couldn't even mount a Christian rock band or a radio or television station to beam God's praise.

A Sustainable Future

ACCOUNTABILITY

Every great theologian has found that ultimate and penultimate security is what makes someone or something one's god. Luther, for example, argues that the heart is a "factory unceasingly fashioning idols" to satisfy needs for certainty and comfort. In his *Catechisms*, he speaks of "having no other gods" and of "having a god" as the process of securing one's being and living. Translated into the crisis I seek to understand, we yearn to trust the provider and the provision of the goods that make our lives safe, content, and happy. Oil is thus elevated to the status of *ersatz* deity. The fact that we would sacrifice thousands of our sons and daughters on battlefields whose wars are primarily about safeguarding access to oil would seem to prove this thesis. In *Bad Money*, Phillips ponders the mania for oil supremacy, the consumer culture, and the lengths we will go to secure this good as a theological heresy of radical religion.[37] Are we like the farmer who took his ease when he had filled his granary only to be shattered by the divine call, "this night your soul (life) will be required of you and what

37. Phillips, *Bad Money*, 89–95.

then of your security?"(Luke 12.20)? Phillips cautions this Puritan nation from idolizing the gods of material things as our lasting security.[38]

At this point, a caution derived from Reinhold Niebuhr is essential to my line of empirical problem diagnosis. A state or nation, a government or corporation is not an individual person. While virtues of love and sacrifice might be applicable to persons, these values may not apply to public collectives and impersonal organizations and industries. Even justice in terms of forgiving transgressions, correcting inequality, and taking preferential options for the poor may be possible more at the interpersonal level than by a social and political organization. Responsibility is different for cities, states, nations, and the international sphere. Here, in the words of Islam is *Dar al-Harb*, not *Dar al-Islam*—the place of war, not peace.

Bill McKibben has written of a sustainable future that it is primarily a matter of conjecture and hope—though averting calamity is more concrete, a radical imperative, it is equally elusive. When we know the data of the carbon footprint, global warming, and ballooning finance, why is it that we cannot help ourselves? This may be a realm where we need international law that always stands in contradiction to our more opportunistic and optimistic states.

OUR PLACE IN NATURE

> Our comforting sense of the permanence of our natural world, our confidence that it will change gradually and imperceptibly if at all, is the result of a subtly warped perspective. Changes that can affect us can happen in our lifetime in our world—not just changes like wars, but bigger and more sweeping events. I believe that without recognizing it we have already slipped over the threshold of such a change, that we are at the end of nature. By the end of nature I do not mean the end of the world. The rain will still fall and the sun shine, though different than before. When I say "nature," I mean a certain set of human ideas about the world and our place in it.[39]

As I ponder in this essay the place of America in the world, McKibben's discussion of "our place in nature" is fundamental. He also affirms what I have called the distortion in our worldview and belief system that underlies the country's apathy and overt harmfulness. As a naturalist, as opposed to a theologian, he has different views of the resilience, recoverability, and ulti-

38. Ibid, 120.
39. McKibben, *The End of Nature*, 7.

mately the redemption of nature. I do concur with McKibben, however, on the occurrence and gravity of our sin and our responsibility.

The crucial importance of my meditation and ideation on the national and global crisis is further developed by McKibben:

> ...an idea, a relationship can go extinct, just like an animal or plant. The idea in this case is "nature," the separate and wild province, the world apart from man to which he adapted, under whose rules he was born and died. In the past, we spoiled and polluted parts of that nature, inflicted environmental damage. But that was like stabbing a man with toothpicks: though it hurt, annoyed, degraded, it did not touch vital organs, block a path of lymph or blood. We never thought that we had wrecked nature. Deep down, we never thought we could: it was too big and too old; its forces—the wind, rain, and the sun—were too strong, too elemental. But, quite by accident, it turned out that the CO_2 and other gasses we were producing in our pursuit of a better life...could alter the power of the sun, could increase its heat. And that increase could change the CO_2—we are ending nature.[40]

Of course it is a bit audacious to assert that we can or could "end nature." God alone is the Creator, Sustainer, and Consummator of nature—including human nature. Where McKibben is totally accurate and prophetic is that in our freedom we are given responsibility and power to steward and shepherd the creation toward its fruitfulness and ability to provide for all creaturely needs. "He opens His hand and fulfills the desire of every living thing ..." (Ps 145.16).

So it is Thanksgiving—a quintessential American holy day. The Puritans invented it in thanks for this new land and deliverance from the old. The holiday was about the foundling nation—and the native one they scarcely realized they were removing. Colonials dwell on grace, not disgrace.

And amid the global exuberance at the prospect of new government in the U.S., the economic sky is falling, the financial system is freezing up like the onrushing winter, and the provident cornucopia of life is drying up. But are we thankful? You bet!—even more so.

POSSIBILITY FOR RENEWAL

My family has lost more this year than it has earned. Our savings, pension, investments, and home-value are down 30 to 40 percent—just this

---

40. Ibid, 41.

year—and compared to us, the poor and disadvantaged are really hurting. Jobs are being lost by the millions as employment is collapsing regionally (*e.g.*, the auto industry in Detroit), nationally, and globally. In a double and triple whammy, resources to help the needy at city, state, and national levels are hard pressed. The state of Illinois—the home of Lincoln and Obama—has pretty much shut down. We are $5 billion in arrears and cannot pay our bills. Children's services, healthcare services, and unemployment insurance fail, and public agencies simply turn people away. Educational institutions wither as funding—especially for poor districts—suffer. College endowments lie devastated.

But we remain thankful—perhaps there is even a turkey in the oven, stuffing on the stove, and pumpkin-pie to boot—and a prayer for the less fortunate and for the ill and elderly who may not survive the winter. *Les Glaneurs* around the world now glean from the edges of fields and garbage heaps scraps of maize and beans—the ancient mandate of Torah and Prophet—that "there shall be no poor among us"(Deut 15.4, Lev 19.10). And we ask again whether our greed and violence, inequality and injustice have brought this about by creating non-viable peaks and intensifications of inhumanity. Are we culpable and therefore responsible and capable of renewal, or is the world just like this?

CONCLUSION

I have delineated the issues of a crisis in America's understanding of its place in God's world. This foundation provides the starting point for an analysis of a defective theology contributing to each particular problem and to the general malaise. Guided by leading social theologians, a constructive theological corrective is then explored. Finally, I delve into concrete pragmatic proposals and spell out a recommendation for renewed theology and programmatic policy in our nation's political life.

2

Contours of a Deficient Theology and Ethics

SECURITY

Imperialism

Emerging Conflicts Around the World

Thanksgiving Day. Americans settle back to turkey, pumpkin pie, and cranberries—blissfully forgetful of the Native peoples they nearly exterminated who first shared these bountiful gifts with them. At this meal, we give thanks for our rapidly diminishing prosperity and hope that the winless Detroit Lions can defeat the near-perfect Tennessee Titans in the football game—a symbol of ever-hoped-for underdog vs. top-dog possibility. While the myths of Captain America and Horatio Alger lie in tatters, the local FM radio station plays Charles Ives's "Variations on America," and the frightful news from Mumbai begins to unfold.

Americans and Brits reportedly were targeted at the Taj Mahal and Oberoi Hotels and at the train station and the Jewish Center. Especially troubling was the taking of hostages at the Chabad House in the Jewish Center—where Brooklyn Rabbi Gavriel Holzberg and his family were killed. The rapid synchronic attacks with bombs, AK-47s, and grenades appears to have been brought about by a group called *Lashkar-e-Taiba* (soldiers of the pure), who were responsible for (in early reports) killing 200 and wounding 400. The 10 terrorists apparently mounted the elaborate sea attack with a large and small ship, perhaps from Pakistan.

Lashkar (LET) is a militant group with a history going back to the Taliban, Afghanistan, and especially, Kashmir. Unspeakable Hindu/Muslim conflict in India has tracked that of the Jewish/Muslim conflict in Palestine for half a century. A *Jihadist* theological, political, and action group, LET claims that its local purpose is to protect the homeland from danger, attack, invasion, and occupation. Abroad, they exert an action strategy designed to destabilize the society and economy of adversaries such as India, Israel, Britain, and America. Disrupting tourism and diverting national commonwealth funds away from human needs to military and security budgets accomplishes this subverting purpose.

India is a democratic nation of 850 million Hindus and 150 million Muslims and Christians. A former Pakistan Ambassador has claimed that the inquiry into Mumbai must consider that the root cause of the attack was the grievance of Indian occupation of Kashmir and the denial of human rights to the country's 120 million Muslims. Meanwhile Indian soldiers have attacked LET cells in Kashmir, finding some who have been accused of involvement in Mumbai.

But why does Pakistan allow such cells? Again America is implicated in the ISI (Pakistani Inter-services Intelligence) investigation into the incident. In a day when the British empire is defunct, and Muslim and American imperial expressions are faltering—a day when *imperium* means economic and political as well as religious and military domination—Kashmir, along with Palestine and the broad horizon of Africa, may be the test cases of whether repressive hegemony or reciprocal liberty will win the day.

The partition of Pakistan in 1947 and the endurance of this land for 60 years as an epicenter of terrorism also is implicit in the atrocity of November 27th in Mumbai. The nascent home of Indo-European, Hindu, and Buddhist faith and life-ways, this nation—along with America and Israel—will test the viability of the covenant of peoples with God and of derivative justice, compassion, freedom, and peace.

Religious Identity in Modern Empires

Why are Americans, the British and religious Jews targeted? Why do they hate us? In America, a refrain of unbelief has resounded for seven years, since the events of September 11th—indeed, since we became a world empire after WW II. Perhaps we need to recall also that Mohandas Gandhi stood against the same Anglo-American empire in its power and wealth from this same land half a century ago. He also sought to bridge Hindu, Christian, and Muslim sensibilities.

And what are the implications of the increasing impossibility of contemporary Jews living peaceful lives in Muslim lands? Once-impressive populations of Jews in cities like Cairo, Mumbai, and Marrakesh have dwindled to dozens. These same Muslim cities that once protected their Jewish urban neighbors now turn against them.

This phenomenon of religious identity in modern empires brings considerable challenge to find cause and cure. Will nations be able to shape peoples of religious identity and character—quintessential qualities required for humanity, justice, and peace—and at the same time forge religiously tolerant communities in which interfaith life can flourish, the quality most necessary to ground freedom?

An example of such justice and concord is found in Rabbi Menachem Froman—an Amos-like visage and justice-soul that is fitting for his home-village of Tekoa—who serves an Orthodox settlement at the edge of the Judean desert. Breaking with his hard-line and implacable congregation, he has spent thousands of hours in interfaith trialogue seeking what he calls the "messianic peace of Jerusalem."[1]

After the Mumbai calamity, another amazing moment of grace and justice came to light. At the Chabad House, Rabbi Gavriel and his family were cruelly and unconscionably tortured and murdered by the criminals. The toddler son of Rabbi Gavriel and mother Rikva was in the next room with his Indian nanny. When the murderers demanded that she come out with the little boy, that they might kill them, she held the child to her breast, defied them to their face, and walked down the stairs. The lad will stay in the care of his great uncle, who runs an orphanage also sponsored by Chabad that serves 7,000 Indian children. The nanny was celebrated at the funeral several days later in a small town near Tel Aviv.

The world is called to protect and safeguard the state of Israel and the Jewish people throughout the world. We have a correlative responsibility to vehemently denounce anyone who would kill any person—certainly for reason of their faith tradition—whether Jewish, Christian, Muslim, Hindu, or of any other faith. We should vow to defend with our lives the right of all persons—regardless of gender, sexual preference, race, age, or faith—to live and thrive in freedom, justice, and peace. The global crisis I address in this essay must not be allowed to pull the world into the pits of such fratricide—which is nothing less than inhumanity, blasphemy, violation of the Spirit of God, and damnation. The only answer is for *Terra Sancta* to again become God's place. Martin Buber captured the vision when he

1. Isabel Kershner, "From an Israeli Settlement, a Rabbi's Unorthodox Plan for Peace," *The New York Times*, December 6, 2008), A8.

saw that Zion could come only as a confraternity of Jew, Christian, and Muslim—in concert with all the companion faiths of the world.[2]

LEGITIMACY OF EMPIRE

These introductory reflections raise religious and ethical questions about the legitimacy of empire. In the Abrahamic faiths, two assertions guide the faithful in their political formulations, economic arrangements, and military endeavors. In the first case, God alone is Lord of life and sovereign over the people. This assertion requires a certain disenchantment and attenuation of the state—especially in its idolatrous pretensions. In the second case, the public and political manifestations of the common life and covenant must become obedient and bring honor to God. At this point, the ambiguities of empires arise. If Yahweh, Christ, or Allah is sovereign over public life and nations, does this imply that the desire of nations will yield theocracy or democracy? Reflecting these ambiguities are the quandaries of identity of the ancient and modern nations of Israel; of the Constantinian, Holy Roman, crusader empires, and movements of Christendom; of Muslim conquests and modern Shariah states.

The background setting of each Abrahamic faith-origin is an inimical, deicidal empire: Egypt, Assyria, Babylon, Greece, and Rome for Israel; Rome for Christianity; and Holy Roman for Islam. All three movements express much of the substance of their respective faiths as *Auseinandersetzung* ("over againstness") to these empires. At the same time, each religious movement itself has taken on aspects of aggressive empire when historical conditions allowed. The heresy of triumphalism often has displaced the righteousness of servitude.

THE ETHICS OF EMPIRE

Thinking of empire as a matter of theological and ethical analysis is a fascination *au courant*. In *The Sorrows of Empire*, Chalmers Johnson says that the events of September 11th prompted some American leaders to see our republic as "a new Rome, the greatest colossus in history, no longer bound by international law, the concern of allies, or any constraints on its use of military force."[3] And in an address at West Point weeks before leaving office, President Bush reaffirmed the Bush Doctrine, contend-

---

2. See Buber, *On Zion.*

3. Johnson, *The Sorrows of Empire*, 3.

ing that America is bestowed with a unique calling requiring us to take force against our enemies (preemptive strikes) before they attack us. With Mumbai fresh in our minds, his words found wide concurrence among the American populace.

Dominic Crossan has written an excellent overview of New Testament perspectives on the ethics of empire.[4] Crossan finds the biblical witness firmly set against such adulation of empire: Jesus clearly posits his kingdom over against the kingdoms and powers of this world. In his classic treatment of Christ and power, *Christ: A Crisis in the Life of God* and in *God: A Biography*, Jack Miles finds a transmutation in the very being of God, from the warrior God of Hebrew scripture—even the sublime God disengaged from our war-making—into the mind and will of God, the Father of Jesus Christ.[5] Theologically speaking, the notion of empire has become pejorative. The thesis I explore goes beyond this dismissal and affirms that each nation and each configuration of nations needs to be responsible to its constituent people, to the world community of peoples, and to God. Global *realpolitik*, juxtaposed between aggressive imperialism and passive isolationism, occurs ultimately within this divine milieu.

In this vein, John Calvin claimed to his student ministers that when all was said and done, they had to be knowledgeable in only two areas: the history of Israel and the history of the Church. Calvin's greatest student—Karl Barth—held the book of the world (newspaper) in one hand and the book of God (scripture) in the other. In my view, the history of God and the history of the world are dialectically and dynamically correlated. The crucial issue is not empire or non-empire, but what is done with powers and prerogatives, resources and influences, capacities and opportunities belonging to each nation. That responsibility requires equality and justice for one's own people and other peoples of the world—all before the One God who owns, supplies, and judges the world.

Empire is inimical to the will and way of God in its demand for ultimate and total allegiance and in its obdurate purpose to obliterate any other entity that might usurp such authority. Despite Paul the Apostle's irenic salutation and appeal to the Roman empire for protection, Christian tradition has on the whole been skeptical of earthly authority, though occasionally lapsing into imperial and triumphal formats herself. Rome

4. See Crossan, *God and Empire*.

5. See Miles, *Christ* and *God*.

crucified Jesus of Nazareth and Peter of Capernaum, stoned to death the Lord's brother, James of Jerusalem, and exiled John of Patmos.

Matthew's Gospel claims that the powers of the world persecuted and killed the prophets (Matt 5.12, 23.31), and that martyrdom remains the cost of witness (Matt 16.24). This teaching would seem to be framed against the threatening background of empire.

Empire is alluring and seductive. Far from the Manichaean "evil empire" of the Bush Doctrine, empire is tantalizing and, in social Darwinian terms, irresistible. A power vacuum occurs in the world when one or several superpowers are missing (*e.g.*, Cold-War Détente). Using analogies from the animal world, the lion must play king even if he is Disney's gentle reluctant occupant of the throne. Studies such as Timo Eskola's *Messiah and the Throne* speak to the incompatability of empire with Abrahamic monotheism and messianism.[6]

EMPIRE AND GOD'S WAY IN THE WORLD

Dominic Crossan delineates this theological dialectic of empire. In *God and Empire*, he outlines four biblical scenarios that lay out scripture's understanding of God's way in the world and human digression from that way. In the section of the book entitled "God and the Ambiguity of Power," he develops four themes from Genesis: divine power in the setting-forth of creation; human derivative power and responsibility in and for that creation; the human misappropriation, usurpation, and misdirection of that cooperative power; and the divine response to the wrong turn and promise of renewal. His stages include:

- The primacy of distributive justice (Genesis 1);
- Responses of human morality (Genesis 2);
- The tragedy of the inaugural fratricide (Genesis 4); and
- Divine punishment and the new beginning (Genesis 6–9).[7]

PRIMACY OF DISTRIBUTIVE JUSTICE

Genesis 1 juxtaposes creation and Sabbath. The priests who compose this material know that making the world "good" is holy gift, worthy of worship. Creation means sacred art and act. Though sublimely free and cre-

---

6. See Eskola, *Messiah and the Throne*.

7. Crossan, *God and Empire*, 50–74.

ative, it is not haphazard trial and error. It is restful contemplation—from everlasting to everlasting. It is evocative and beatific: Praise is shown forth and exultation is offered in return.

The essence of Sabbath is the pause to glorify as one is glorified: "God opens his hand and satisfies the desire of every living thing" (Ps 145.16). The striking aspect of God's self-rest is that it is shared with each and every creature: ". . .your slaves, your children, your donkey and goat, even the refugee in your town" (Deut 5.14). It thus becomes a work of justice and equality. Indeed justice is the substance of creation as creation is the vehicle of justice.

The meaning of this crucial point for my thesis is that power is profuse and diffuse—meant to be shared, not concentrated.[8] Distributive justice is the divine gift enabled through human implementation. Power is in service to redemption: It exists for the empowerment of the creation, of each creature. It cannot be restricted to personal or national purpose. It cannot be contorted from edification to domination. Here the nuance of my thesis becomes clear. Empire is not, *per se*, wrong. It becomes wrong and dangerous as it betrays the purpose of power—which is divine justice showered and distributed on each and every creature.

RESPONSES OF HUMAN MORALITY

Genesis 2 comes from an older stratum of literary tradition that reflects an ancient and universal understanding about the human condition and human behavior. The portrayal includes what can best be described as an empirical report of what humans are really like in nature and action. Observation shows that we are free and responsible—able to know options and to choose—and that we resist authority, even rightful and wise counsel. Choosing rather to go against our finer nature, we turn self-destructive and violent.

The story of the fall (Gen 2.3b–3.24) concerns our primordially ordained knowledge of good and evil followed by deliberate disavowal of that charter mandate, even though we know full-well the consequences of disobedience. A very subtle and difficult insight into the human condition arises at this point. It is expressed in the dictum of Paul the Apostle, Augustine, and Luther: *non posse non peccata* ("it is impossible not to sin," cf. Augustine, Sermon 99). Are self-aggrandizement and injustice

---

8. See Migliore, *The Power of God*.

inescapable human conditions inevitably made manifest in individual and collective action, or are persons capable of being and doing good? I personally believe humans are capable of righteous and just being and activity—a conviction I come to by virtue of God's bestowal of Torah and Gospel, which surely cannot be futile or impossible gifts. Still the inveterate Calvinist in me feels the compelling truth of Reinhold Niebuhr—that sin is the most empirically verifiable fact about the human race.

If this is the case, then imperial ambition will always provoke ethical challenge. The Darwinian paradigm—determinative in much political, economic, and military life—must be placed in dialogue with the theistic paradigm if there is to be truth, justice, and peace in the world. As Alain Badiou showed in *Metapolitics*, injustice is easier to define than justice, violence easier than peace.[9] A full-orbed understanding necessary for conviction and action requires polity and theology.

Tragedy of Inaugural Fratricide

Genesis 4 works out this seemingly inevitable tragedy in stories such as Cain and Abel, eventually elaborated in the historical and antediluvian narrative of the Tower of Babel (Gen 11). Here we find the normative structure given to help us fathom the phenomenon of imperial activity in world history. In unbounded hubris, we turn against our fellow-humans, believing that our superiority demands the subordination or elimination of others. The progression of imputed or implicated injustice involves disbelief, denial, and finally rage and shame at being singled out from among the wide company of sinners—caught, accused, and convicted. The paradigmatic strife between rancher and farmer in scripture is perfectly reenacted in the litanies of Wall Street or the now evacuating "finance fantasies" of London and New York. The self-justifying cry remains the same: "Am I my brother's keeper?" Inhumanity flows from delusions of grandeur. The *Sanhedrin* portion of Talmud asks why in Adam God created only one man. The answer: God created only one man so that no one could say "my God is greater than your God."

Throughout Crossan's discussion of this topic, an ethical subtlety is present. The choice before these primal proto-humans involves choosing eternal life or death, the former demanding obedience (and that we ask no questions), the latter entailing the receipt of moral knowledge, but

---

9. See Badiou, *Metapolitics*.

also damnation. We may wonder whether we are dealing in the "Fall" with descent or ascent. The perennial lure of the tree of knowledge and the tree of life seems to involve a bondage and servitude, bringing salvation on the one hand and a liberation entailing death on the other.

Granted, a great theological gulf exists on the point between Judaism and Christianity and between the Athanasian and Arian and the Calvinist and Arminian versions of the Christian faith. Nevertheless a perceptive read of the varying dialectical theological moods of the faith allows for a paradoxical commingling where human initiative, freedom, and creativity coexist in synergy with life under God as bounded obedience. In public life, as opposed to personal ethics, this insight might foster certain autonomies in the public sphere Reinhold Niebuhr would call "realism." In this context, even temporary and provisional hegemony might be acceptable, stopping short of the invasion and occupation of empire. The U.S. now considers this course in Congo, Mali, and Chad in order to check internal and infiltrating violence.

DIVINE PUNISHMENT AND THE NEW BEGINNING

Crossan summarizes his analysis of empire critique from Genesis with a discussion of the deeply ambivalent and troubling Noah-Abram narrative in which God decides that earthly iniquity is so far advanced that he will obliterate all of humanity (except one righteous family) in a sin-flood: "... and the Lord God was sorry that he made humankind on the earth" (Gen 6.6). Then follows the destructive taking back of creation as each creative day is undone for it was bad—very bad: "... I will blot out all the creatures I have created—birds, animals, all creeping things" (Gen 6.7). But the outrage and terrible retribution is short-lived: "Never again will I destroy ..." A renewed covenant is offered to Noah and his family, again reinstituting the creation: "Be fruitful and multipl ..." and to Abraham: "I will bless you and make you great" (Gen 7–12).

The inner lineaments of these great texts prove that divine punishment actually conceals mercy, and that destruction actually is a declaration that justice is the essential meaning of creation. Continuing Torah makes clear that creation obviates empire and transmutes aggressive human domination into a new covenant of justice and equality. Here and now, debts are remitted (Deut 15.1–2); slaves are freed (Deut 21.7–11); dispossession is reversed (Deut 25.10); and in a just and equal distribution of land-as-life, pristine creation is reinstated. The destructive interlude of inter-human aggression, greed, and domination has not been allowed to prevail and despoil the good. Creation now and ever-after will be a platform of messianic justice, deliverance, and jubilee. Human intention to establish a twisted creation of greed, domination, inhumanity, and earth destruction—though persistent and ubiquitous—will not prevail. The good earth belongs to God and his companion, the bread of life. God's people on earth are given mandate to make this happen, and the perennial Logos assures that their actions will not be in vain.

Hegemony

ALTRUISM OR SELF-AGGRANDIZEMENT?

Hegemony is a broader cognate phenomenon of distorted theology of creation relating to oppression or subordination of others brought about by a range of powers expressed singly or in concert. While it lacks the theological provocation of empire, it also is a value-laden process. Economic, military, and political measures often are employed to influence or impose one nation's will on others. In the most favorable light, hegemony can simply mean exerting influence based on the positive traits in one's tradition. At root, the phenomenon is morally neutral if it takes place in the context of the wide-ranging exchange of ideas and convictions. If one nation's products win out over others in the free marketplace, that ought to be well and good. But if coercion, controlled media, imposed authority, terror, even unfair competition bring about the injustice of hegemony, the practice becomes suspect.

Here we begin to see the complexity of the issue. There are no such things as totally free markets, marketplaces of ideas, or political public-squares or town meetings. In the words of the old adage—"money talks." The disadvantaged are always at a disadvantage. The world is not a utopia. Sound international policy requires assertion for good from the benefits and resources of each nation given over to the whole human community. Love of neighbor as an international expression also requires restraint from wrong-doing and the recognition of mutual and reciprocal contributions of every nation in God's world.

Such a foreign policy posture can be found in America's approach to Germany and Japan during and after WWII. Theologian-ethicist Donald Shriver develops a responsible version of that leadership in his broader study on the importance of forgiveness in international affairs.[10] Biblical doctrine counsels:

> To everything there is a season,
> And a time for every purpose under the sun...
> A time to kill and a time to heal ...
> A time to love and a time to hate;
> A time for war and a time for peace (Eccl 3.1–8).

In the same way that Cyrus the Persian was called *Ebed Yahweh*—the messianic servant—to deliver Israel/Judah from Babylonian captivity (I Esd 2.3), Shriver shows how America was called on to serve in the sacrificial delivery of Europe and Asia from fascism. The structure and substance of what would become the world's next empire was, in that moment, given over to the God of justice and peace. It was not until the next travail of history—the conflict with communism—that U.S. policy would succumb to the theological distortions of empire and move toward the pretensions, audacities, and idolatries of the later twentieth century in Asia (*e.g.*, Vietnam) and South America (*e.g.*, Nicaragua). Then the full-blown theological distortion became clear.

In the historical context of the 1930s and 1940s, power was exerted to resist and then restore enemies—true redemption. In the 1960s and 1970s, empire became an end in itself and our "security" and "national interest"—euphemisms for vested self-interest—true damnation.

Hegemony, defined as one party leading along the federation of affected parties in achieving liberation from oppression, can be offered altruistically, with no vested interest, or hegemonically, in the more pejorative sense where the real objective proves to be self-aggrandizement.

In the challenges that scripture calls "temptations," history leads all of the world's peoples into times and seasons for building up and for tearing down. To be good and godly, a hegemon must become servant and seek to bring down only when it is the necessity of building up. Like imperial power, caution must be exercised in hegemonic intervention because of the great capacity humans have for self-deception. When imperial ambition is transformed into the search for the kingdom of God, its justice among humanity, and righteousness for all creation—that theological error has discovered truth and peace. "Righteousness and justice are the foundation of thy throne; steadfast love and faithfulness go before thee"

---

10. See Shriver, *An Ethic for Enemies.*

(Ps 89.14). When hegemony seeks not its own but the good of others, it too has transformed that lethal distortion.

To sum up this reflection on the modalities of power labeled empire and hegemony, especially as they manifest in what I have termed distorted or deficient theology, I offer a seasonal meditation on the meaning of power. Gian Carlo Menotti wrote the opera "Amahl and the Night Visitors" after viewing the haunting painting by Hieronymous Bosch, "Adoration of the Shepherds." A desperately poor Bedouin mother and her disabled son are visited under the Bethlehem star by the three kings. Dazzled by their grandeur and the costly gifts, she steals the gold as the Magi rest. Caught red-handed, the gift for the Christ-child is wrested from the sobbing mother. King Melchoir sings of the promised child, of real power, and of that enduring kingdom:

> Woman, you may keep the gold. The child we seek doesn't need
>   our gold.
> On love, on love alone, He will build his Kingdom.
> His pierced hand will hold no scepter. His hallowed head will wear
>   no crown.
> His might will not be built on your toil.
> Swifter than lightening, He will soon walk among us.
> He will bring us new life and receive our death.
> And the keys to His Kingdom belong to the poor.
> . . . Let us leave my friends.[11]

As they depart, the lame lad says "take my crutch, the child may need it." And he walks . . . he walks . . . to travel to Bethlehem with the Kings.

A Chosen People

Chosenness as Self-Adulation

There may not be a more despised person in the world. As representative leader of the most feared nation in the world, he is blamed, rightly or wrongly, for the deaths of tens of thousands of Iraqis, the exile of millions of Palestinians, and the economic disaster now affecting the entire world population. When 28-year-old Iraqi journalist Muntaner al-Zaidi threw his shoes at President Bush and shouted in Arabic: "This is a gift from the Iraqis; this is the farewell kiss you dog!"—it seemed like Kruschevian

11. "Amahl & the Night Visitors" soundtrack, RCA, 1990 (compact disc).

or Castro-like harmless vehemence. The farewell news conference in Baghdad was meant to celebrate the newly signed security agreement between the U.S. and Iraq to maintain bases while otherwise "going away." The event came at a "perfect-storm" moment when American weariness and Iraqi discontent commingled to bring our invasion and occupation to an end. Al-Zaidi was beaten and hauled off to jail amid national adulation. The president deftly ducked the two-missile attack with moves we would expect from a Texas baseball man.

Part of the global contempt for Bush is that he sees himself as "a chosen instrument"[12] sent from a chosen people. All the while "paradise-destined" suicide bombers marshal their havoc on Sunni and Shia populations who each, in turn, have their own divine pretensions. The ultimate fallacy of power with deep and misguided theological undertones is the notion of a chosen people. When the self-esteem of one's community as chosen becomes self-adulation—"my strength has gotten me this wealth" (Deut 8.17)—empire and hegemony pale in comparison. There is much danger and potency in the conviction that one is a "divine instrument."

Trouble ensues when national sociopolitical groups, in many cases groups alienated from the cognate theocentric communities, take up the torch of chosenness and cause havoc. Pub-stool drunkards in Dublin and Belfast become flaming patriots; a belligerent and Islamophobic state of Israel Army and secret service proceed as if they were the chosen ones; *Hamas* or *Hezbollah* pretend to bear the sacred cause; and American politicians similarly delude themselves. Even Robert Mugabe—like Stalin, Hitler, or Saddam Hussein—fails to see that he is the very demonic antithesis of the divine deliverer he perceives himself to be. The Emperor Constantine is no longer Paul the Apostle, and Francis of Assisi praying "peace be upon you" is not Pope Urban II shouting "God wills it." Benjamin Netanyahu is not Martin Buber, and Suleiman the Great at the gates of Vienna is not the Prophet Muhammad, weaponless en transit from Medina to Mecca.

Chosenness as Stewardship

Being chosen, however, has two meanings—one is negative, a usurpation, and the other positive, a divine calling. Nations in biblical purview either choose a role of being superior or being servant peoples. This section ex-

---

12. Oliver Stone, *W.*, IGN Movies, 2008.

plores these two modes of living with power in God's world. Messianic peoplehood follows the latter form: "Behold my servant, in whom I delight" (Isa 42.1). A strenuous claim on the theme of chosenness in the Judaic tradition emphasizes that it does not mean superiority. This historic people are singled out from many far greater peoples to partner with Yahweh in a peculiar covenant. Torah and *Tanakh*—the oral-become-literary constitution of this people—defines and describes this covenant. From the beginning, the two-way understanding of life together has meant demand as much as favor. "You are a holy people to YHWH your God. God has chosen you to be his treasured people from all peoples on the face of the earth" (Deut 14.2). "You only have I singled out of all the families on earth. Therefore I will visit upon you all your iniquities" (Amos 3.2). Separation for holiness and judgment on wrong-doings?—these are not necessarily welcome gifts.

This covenantal complexity begins the conviction that chosenness is a mixed blessing at best. It certainly does not imply privilege, protection, favoritism, and superiority. In heavy irony, feeling chosen may indeed be the compensatory mechanism of peoples whose very existence is constantly threatened. The unique cultural gift Jews bring to the world is ironic joy—the taste and hope of yearned-for days of happiness and peace—perfectly understandable for a people who have watched one of every two ancestors (back to the messiah Jesus) being killed before their lives were lived out.

The people of Israel are trustees or stewards of the Word and Law of God. They have been chosen to receive and bear a message. This is a sacred witness, meaning nothing less than attestation of life that may well lead to death. The poor and needy hear this Word gladly. The smug and rich despise it and are infuriated. Jews as idolaters, war-mongers, adulterers, greed-seekers, and those who degrade the poor impede the progression of Word into the world and disgrace their Lord and their calling. The same is true for the sibling faith-families of Christianity and Islam. Election and vocation—Torah—is yoke and burden, light and easy since Messiah is the main puller, but yoke and burden nevertheless. This image is replete in early Jewish and Christian literature (*e.g.*, Matt 11.29–30). The chosen are servants *of*, not superiors *to* the Word.

The idea of chosen people introduces a most-dangerous theological idea into history, bringing about concrete military, economic, political, even religious phenomenon that adversely affect God's world and the divine redemption of justice, love, and peace within that cosmos. Scriptural history and the theological traditions of faith come to condemn this—the usurping and corrupting of a divine vocation into human ambition and malice—as idolatry and injustice, provoking a Noachic judgment of God through the vehicles of natural and political history.

"Hear this, you who swallow up the needy, even to make the poor of the land to fail. When will the new moon and the Sabbath be over so we can return to buying the poor for silver and the needy for a pair of shoes?... Shall not the land tremble for this?" (Amos 8.4–6). When the Torah of human justice and compassion is set aside to make way for human pretension, injustice, and projected, presumed chosenness—the land trembles.

ECONOMY

Radical Religion

A DEFECTIVE THEOLOGY

Kevin Phillips uses the term "radical religion" to characterize what I am calling defective theology. The same suspicious faith he found mischievously at work in *The Cousins' Wars*—bringing about a dark side to the small measure of nobility found in the English Civil War, the American Revolution, and the American Civil War—was a radical, perhaps "retrograde" religion.[13] In his recent set of books about the spiritual and ethical fallacy embedded in the crisis of America in world history, he seems to confront what might better be called "American Triumphalism" or "American Theocracy."[14] What is the religious culture and mentality of which he speaks?

The "Bad God" behind "Bad Money" is variously defined as "Christian Fundamentalism," the "Evangelical preoccupation with personal salvation," and a widespread God-wants-you-to-be-rich prosperity gospel. Phillips continues: "... forty percent of those who voted for Bush in 2000 and 2004 put aside their populist economics, which described their parents and grandparents in Oklahoma and the Dakotas ...." They voted "their new preoccupation ... to concentrate on Jesus their redeemer, to imbibe fear of Islam, to watch a crescendo of seeming biblical prophesy unfold with a roar in the Middle East .... The place to start was with

13. See Phillips, *The Cousins' Wars*.
14. See Phillips, *American Theocracy* and *American Dynasty*.

Bullnomics" (Madoff), market worship, and an idolatry "of the financial ideology."[15]

As much as I concur with these sentiments, I must point out that it is poor religious sociology. This described theology is pure idolatry and not the indigenous faith that evangelized America—the faith of Calvin, the Puritans, Baptists, and Wesleyans. That is, unless—and this may be the case—these immigrant faiths were corrupted with cultural heresies that tore them away from the theocentric theologies and justice ethics of those constituting faith heritages.

In *Fiddler on the Roof*, Tevye speaks for everyman when he asks, "would it disturb some great almighty plan, if I were a wealthy man?" Convictions oscillate wildly within the Weberian economic/theological ethos. At the same time, poverty is a sign of dereliction and prosperity a sign of righteousness. In the U.S., as we approach the new year of 2009, great wealth has become a sign of disrepute. No more "golden parachutes" for corrupt CEOs. Wall Street is now a place of sacrilege. Even the heroic aura of September 11th has evaporated like the dusty mist. Hank Paulson took a $.5 billion separation package when he left Goldman. And great disgrace! The big three auto CEOs took private jets to beg Congress, "tin-cup in hand," for a bail-out.

It is the first day of winter (20 degrees below zero in Chicago) and the first night of Hanukkah. Reflection remains roiled in Santa land. In this season, one might say that all religion has a healthy dose of fantasy and fabrication—some society for truth in New York City shows conclusively that angels do not exist. This I will not dispute. As Luther exposited in his *Catechism*, "The human heart is the factory of idols." My goal in this essay is to show the earth-changing impact of this cultural fabrication. What Freud, Marx, Nietzsche, and Feuerbach call "false religion" is at the very heart of the global crisis we address: economic, political, and military.[16]

President Bush asks this holiday season what he did wrong to throw the world into economic meltdown and ensure Obama's election. With the accuracy of hindsight, his critics point out his "Santa Claus" paternalism that caused him to imagine erroneously that the best thing for American

---

15. Phillips, *Bad Money*, 72.

16. Feuerbach viewed religion as an "absurdity, a nullity, a pure illusion." Freud, Marx, and Nietzsche—referred to as the "masters of suspicion"—also believed religion to be false, a spiritual problem of some sort: an alienating power (Marx); a sickness (Nietzsche); and a collective neurosis (Freud). See Harvey, *Feuerbach*.

prosperity was people owning their own homes and markets remaining largely unregulated. This fantasy was the cause.[17]

Phillips plies his expertise as a one-time Republican political strategist as he traces the demographics of the last three national elections. In 2008, the country suddenly turned from a red mass with blue slivers on the East and West coasts and along the upper-north-central industrial strip (where suspect Ohio and Florida turned the 2004 tide) now to a blue (or perhaps purple) mass with a big red exception (Central Western, Mormon country, Texas, and Oklahoma) bleeding into a thin red line across Arkansas, Mississippi, Alabama, Georgia, Tennessee, and South Carolina. Phillips asks about the theological ideology that animated this Bush coalition that only Governor Sarah Palin could save from tearing into Confederate tatters.

THE PROSPERITY ERROR

Initially, it was "prosperity-Gospel" country. Calvinists and Wesleyans, Mormons and Pentecostals abound. The prosperity megachurches—Joel Osteen's Lakewood Church in Houston, T.D. Jakes' The Potter's House in Dallas, and Creflo Dollar's World Changers Church International near Atlanta—flourish here. In the inner-Western states, the healthful and industrious Mormons hold sway. Surveys on voter beliefs consistently affirmed that God's wish was prosperity, healing, and miracles for his people. "If you give God money, He will give you money," or as the church van in front of the Pentecostal Afro-Caribbean church near our house proclaims, "As the prayers go up, the blessings come down." All this poor Calvinist preacher can now pray for these struggling saints is "Amen—may it be so!"

Like all heresies, prosperity theology is a partial truth. While I develop a corrective theology in the next section of this study, let us note here that providential theology of creation is the fabric from which is torn the prosperity error. Providence, as I have noted in our discussion of creation and justice, is the doctrine of the Triune God of Israel, Jesus of Nazareth, and Islam—where the dynamics of divine love and judgment are mediated in human life through the vehicles and vicissitudes of nature and history. These impulses affect the sustenance and destiny of the good earth and resident humanity. Though frail and finite, humanity is borne up into the messianic redemption of the world, as Logos, Son, and Savior

17. Jo Becker, et al., "White House Philosophy Stoked Mortgage Bonfire," *The New York Times*, December 21, 2008.

transport the body humane into God's self. Thus, incorporated futility is being transformed into hope of new creation. Such redemption remains cruciform and agonal and not prosperous and successful in worldly terms. We are not promised prosperity, but presence. In sacrificial care for the sick, poor, oppressed, suffering, and vulnerable, the mystery of eschatological renewal is being proleptically performed: "the chastisement of our peace was upon Him and with His wounds we are healed" (Isa 53.5).

THE MANICHAEAN ERROR

Beyond prosperity the prevalent theology is "Manichaean." The construal of good and evil in the operative theology finds focal evil not in Babylon or Rome, not in Pope or Emperor, not in Fascism or Communism, but in global *Jihadic* Islam. From Bush to McCain, the enemy of America in world affairs was "the transcendent evil of militant Islam." Part of the broader fabric of apocalyptic eschatology, an Armageddon full of Israeli/Palestinian connotations is envisioned, indeed yearned for, and helped along wherever possible. Richard Cizik, former president of the National Association of Evangelicals, finds that "Evangelicals have substituted Islam for the Soviet Union as the 'evil empire'—a religion of violence and world-domination."[18]

The error here can only be rectified by rediscovering a sound Christology and axiology. If "antichrist" is misconstrued from the biblical enemies of Christ—famine, war, disease, injustice, ignorance, and oppression—into a prejudice and discrimination like anti-Semitism or Islamophobia, severe repercussions will be felt in world history.

In sum, "radical religion" produces a range of theological errors that ground the military, economic, and environmental crises I call "Bases Abroad," "Bad Money," and "Black Gold." I have noted Manichaeanism in international awareness, prosperity Gospel, and market-worship in economic science—and conscience and a generic apocalyptic, end-of-the-world yearning that mitigates against environmental stewardship. I now examine two additional theological issues that obfuscate salutary commitments to our care for the earth: "The Invisible Hand" and a phenomenon addressed by a phrase from contemporary politics—"Spreading the Wealth."

---

18. Phillips, *Bad Money*, 90.

The Invisible Hand

Freedom and Enterprise

We should not be surprised that heirs of the Scots Calvinists in the America of "W" Bush should fall into the error of "trusting the market." A faith-brother of the old chosen-people covenant and of the new Scots variant, Nobel-prize-winning economist Milton Friedman and his teacher Adam Smith definitively articulated the root religioeconomic concept of the "Invisible Hand."

In a discussion of the underlying virtues and values of domestic and foreign commerce in *The Wealth of Nations*, Adam Smith confesses that he suspects the benevolence of those who find trading with others the best way to serve our neighbors in need. Denying that altruistic action abroad really serves the domestic "common good," he calls for responding to an Invisible Hand—which he firmly believed to be the reality of his Calvinistic God—whereby seeking the most profitable course of action for yourself would enhance that same "happiness" for your proximate neighbors in business and ultimately for your remote neighbors.[19]

In the same vein, Milton Friedman believed that the Invisible Hand was the impulse, force, and spirit assuring the possibility of cooperation without coercion, where each consumer in his freedom brings what he wants to what each producer freely wants to make. Thus, a synergy or symphony of benevolent activity is produced. One can only wonder how such assumptions of human nature and its benevolence arose from the extant notions of human goodness and corruption in this land of Calvin and Knox. It was here, we recall, that not only did the liberal and humanistic institutions—democracy and capitalism—take hold and reach a certain refinement, but also these values were accompanied by a stolid realism about human depravity and exploitation.

Despite their optimism, both Smith and Friedman articulate an expansive philosophy of freedom and enterprise. Smith's classic *The Wealth of Nations*, and other works on moral sentiments, and Friedman's *Capitalism and Freedom* both chart similar directions.[20] In vocational choices, students will freely choose for the neediest professions that will naturally be the most lucrative. Bright students in college now follow course, choosing

---

19. See Smith, *The Wealth of Nations*.
20. See Friedman, *Capitalism*.

medicine, law, and business—and certainly not teaching—until Bernard Madoff, that is. One might wonder if we are in such a late phase of capitalist freedom where the finance sector—the most lucrative—seems to have become the most popular (8 percent in America, 20 percent in Britain), but in many ways also the most superfluous, moving into any niche of potential profit while free capital flows, but disappearing just as rapidly in times of greater equilibrium of goods and services.

International associations are also directed by an Invisible Hand (a kind of natural law) in free-market philosophy. Workers in poor countries are pleased to work cheaply (and without benefits and protections) because this will give them the competitive edge. What could be wrong with Chinese and African workers making Nike basketball shoes the world over? Is this not, theologically speaking, divine providence reducing inequalities across the myriad peopled creation or Messiah making level the ground at the foot of the cross?

In an oft-quoted passage, Adam Smith again challenges the hypocrisy of much altruistic "put on" by the affluent, by pleading that we openly admit that we are self-interested creatures.

> It is not from the benevolence of the butcher, the brewer or the baker that we expect our dinner, but from their regard to their own self-interest. We address ourselves, not to their humanity, but to their self-love, and never talk to them of our own necessities, but of their advantages.[21]

Invisible Hand is shorthand for "the way things work." Smith seems to be saying, waxing a bit theological, that while we might wish people were more generous, that's just human nature. Probably the best thing we can do for this cruel world, where people live in hovels and congregate on grates under the streets for a bit of heat, is seek a life in which rulers and democratic governments provide some floors—orphanages, hospitals, hospices, and the like. Churches also should create lively philanthropic programs as the main public elymosenary arm. Best of all perhaps is that out of homelands like Presbyterian Scotland would arise more capitalist entrepreneurs like Andrew Carnegie and Andrew Mellon to found public schools, colleges, libraries, and jobs in mining and transportation. The Calvinist anthropology we find in Smith is probably something like Ebenezer Scrooge transfigured—where his piles of coins go to help Tiny

---

21. Smith, *The Wealth of Nations*, 315.

Tim's and Cratchit families in need. Such entrepreneurial philanthropists might well embody John Wesley's dictim to "*earn* all you can in order to *save* all you can in order to *give* all you can." Warren Buffett and Bill Gates—here we come.

How, in this era of bad money, has this so sacred theology too become bad? First we need to recognize that the economic and "financial" apparatus has become complex to the point of now being nondescript and indefinable. In his book, *The Great Inflation*, Robert Samuelson records some of these elusive facts:

- Venture capital rose from $18 billion in 1997 to $107 billion in 2000.

- NYSE trading volume rose from 5 million shares a day in 1980 to 2 billion in 2006.

- Morgan-Stanley in 1950 had one office of 100 employees; in 2007 the company was in 333 countries with 47,000 employees.

- In 1946, household debt was 23 percent of family income; in 2006, 134 percent.

- Home ownership in 1940 was 44 percent; in 2007, 68 percent.[22]

An even greater historical span has passed from the late feudal (shops and guilds) and early factory (pin-making) commerce of Adam Smith's day down to ours. The world of broad-scale speculation and massive invention of purely electronic packages of goods requires a transfiguration of Calvin's operational "theatre of God's glory"—as well as his natural law of organized and animated economic cosmos—to one more cosmic such as that of Teilhard de Chardin. The deficiency of the dominant and regnant theology to comprehend and guide such complexity may simply be that it is outmoded. My analysis finds it also to be misguided—taking cues from human malevolence rather than excellence.

The Smith, Hayak, Friedman school of economic philosophy shared the sublime worldview of Calvin where the true, good, and beautiful were synchronic and synergic in realms of human energy and activity such as learning, the professions, science, music, and the arts. Even the "dismal science" of economics took its place in this ethic and aesthetic entourage.[23] The Platonic formula of Keats pertained: "beauty is truth, truth

---

22. Samuelson, *The Great Inflation*, 218.

23. See Vaux, *Birth Ethics* and *Death Ethics*.

is beauty." But economics faltered in failing to keep a prophetic (critical) ethical and theological paradigm central to its disciplinary philosophy. The Invisible Hand beliefs—supply, demand, inflation, unemployment, competition, "survival of the fittest," greed, and avarice—were conceived in Social-Darwinian terms as forces of nature that were fixed and unchanging. Imbued with moral truth—because of our lack of discriminating knowledge about human-projected phenomena that had become unjust and demonic—*stoicha*—"powers of the world" (Col 1.13 and 2.10), the Invisible Hand had become idolatry. Though subtle, the theological error at this point is profound.

The practical policies of classical capitalism also have come under moral and theological scrutiny as public systems and structures—not private—have been found to be more essential to the general well-being. Milton Friedman proposed public policies such as a flat tax, which was never enacted but which moved our U.S. economy radically toward one where the rich retained much more income and a greater portion of income than the working class. This policy generated more and more resentment among poor and middle classes. Friedman policies such as "no minimum wage" and privatization of sectors such as health care, post office, transportation, education, and retirement (pensions) also became more controversial. Though all have been only imperfectly privatized, these as well as the more fully privatized sectors of finance, banking, and corporate life continued to be harmful to public desires and values.

The avarice/opportunism factor of economic phenomenon under private-sector domination was most tragically disclosed in Samuelson's statistics on deferred obligations. In the time-span between 2000 and 2008, Gross Domestic Product grew from $10 to $14 trillion. In the same span, (paralleling private debt) obligations (social security, Medicare, unemployment insurance, etc.) grew from $29 to $70 trillion. The obligations were not paid, but deferred to the future. To this future obligation, we must add Nobel Laureate Joseph Stiglitz' estimate of deferred obligations from the Iraq war (mercenaries, etc.) totaling $3 to $7 trillion.[24]

We had become ambivalent, in other words. We refused to become a complete and consistent Smith/Friedman-type state or a coherently Keynesian state. We were mixed up. Economic sins, it became clear, ulti-

---

24. See Stiglitz and Bilmes, *The Three Trillion Dollar War.*

mately were sins against future generations or to be more blunt—against our children and grandchildren.

So, today Max Weber's U.S.—the world's most heightened and intense capitalist nation—also is the world's greatest debtor nation, rapidly becoming highly state-subsidized and owned. When we appeal non-responsibility to the future as per the old adage, "what did the future ever do for me?" or *Après moi, le déluge*[25]—we need to remember that such disdain for the future has religious roots, especially in more apocalyptic movements. Authentic accountability rather responds to the good of the neighbor transcendentally considered beyond time and space restrictions, as well as in the here and now.

Naïveté about untoward consequences of risk-filled actions—inordinate faith in the future and the trustworthiness of others, a probable biological and neurological propensity to deceive in certain persons, and an almost universal incapability to admit error, apologize, and amend one's ways—compounds to form the theological error of what is called the Invisible Hand. Such a constellation of blind and destructive trust, with heavy doses of exploiting others, makes the candid confessions of Chairman Greenspan before the House Committee on Government Oversight and Reform all the more remarkable. Commenting on the non-regulative premise of "Invisible Hand" economics, he confessed, "I made a mistake in trusting that free markets could regulate themselves without government oversight." A fervent proponent of deregulation in his 18 years as Chair of the Fed, he was reluctant to regulate even the new precarious instruments of derivatives. "I made a mistake in presuming that the self-interests of organizations, specifically banks and others were best capable of protecting their own shareholders and their equity. I have found a flaw and I don't know how significant or permanent it is. For forty years I have been going on considerable evidence that it was working exceptionally well."[26]

A hint at a corrective theology of providence follows these lines. The inescapable arrogance of feeling chosen and of being the receiver of bene-

25. *Après moi, le déluge* is French for "after me comes the flood." Attributed to King of France Louis XV, this phrase expresses the mindset of those who destroy the earth and human life without regard for the future.

26. "Greenspan Admits Flaw to Congress, Predicts More Economic Problems," The Online News Hour, PBS, October 23, 2008, www.pbs.org/newshour/bb/business /july-dec08/crisis_hearing_10-23.html.

fits of an Invisible Hand must be transfigured into responsible Abrahamic humility as we see ourselves as messengers and reflectors—the sands of the sea-shores and the stars of the skies (Gen 22.17 ff). Such servant-hood is only possible as *Akedic* (Isaac/ Ishmael) sonship, messiahship, and Logos cosmology is ventured, displacing violent triumphalism. Only then will we offer ministries of justice in interfaith confraternity to the world that is God's first love. The first quality of this new being will be sacrificial and generous care for this world's poor and needy.

Spreading the Wealth

Sharing and Peacemaking

Laying down those contours of that theological construct I fully offer in Part Three begins here with a consideration of a popular phrase.

Urbi et orbi ("to the city of Rome and to the world"), the Pope's Christmas message from the Vatican, focuses today on transfiguring our human inclination and propensity toward selfishness and careless-ness into sharing and peace-making. The man offers solid counsel—in 62 languages, no less—but is anyone listening? I have on my desk this morning of Christ's Nativity a dialogue before the Catholic Academy of Bavaria between Benedict (then Prefect for the Congregation of the Faith/Inquisition) and renowned philosopher, Jürgen Habermas. Despite good intentions, the two statesmen seem to be talking past each other as they discuss "secularized and Christianized Europe."

The importance, yet seeming irrelevance, of these ships passing in the night becomes clear as the Pope continues his call for church (now obsessed with inner turmoil/cf. the film "Doubt") and state ("how did we get ourselves in this economic fix?") to attend to world problems like Africa—*e.g.*, Zimbabwe, once the breadbasket of Africa and now the festering hell-hole of rampant hunger and cholera. He addressed other myriad places of "interminable sufferings" like Somalia, Sudan, and Israel/ Palestine. Why can't we turn our warring madness and "frenzy of apathy" into the building of peace and stability—the Bethlehem gifts of Church and State? If we continue on this present course, he warns the world will "fall apart." Apropos the 2008 Papal Christmas greeting, columnist Mike Royko once contrasted the motto of Chicago *Urbs in Horto* (city in a park) now become *Ubi est Mea*—(where's mine)—and there's the rub!

The phrase "Spreading the Wealth" became highly politicized during the 2008 presidential campaign. Barack Obama was accused of slapping the "Invisible Hand" that fed him. He was, God forbid, a socialist and communitarian. He had violated his home-base-Milton Friedman school of economics, was making sounds of massive government "stimulus" plans, a new "New Deal." He even favored "bail out" for the big three auto companies in Detroit. The most serious charge was that he believed in a New Testament *koinonia* ethic where all shared in one "Commonwealth" of "spreading" or "sharing" the wealth (Acts 2.42ff). Imagine, here, in Max Weber's nation of maximal capitalist fruition, one challenged the sacred cows of private property, asked again not "what our country could do for us but what we could do for our country" (and world) —and he won!

The message echoed older clarion calls in the Anglo-American tradition. Teddy Roosevelt had boldly demanded that "...we will see that prosperity is shared and we will not allow that swindling investors will take everything from the consumers"—sound familiar? John Maynard Keynes openly advocated pooling capital wealth to achieve justice. America had inherited from England and France the tradition of the "Commons" and the "Commonwealth." The communitarian ethos was exemplified by many groups—Shakers, Quakers, Amish, the Mennonites, Hutterites, and other peace churches. Even radical and primitive communists, socialists, Judaic solidarity proponents, and Utopianists were not unknown.

The age of mid-nineteenth century down to the dawn of the twenty-first century saw the rise of three great economic philosophies: socialism, capitalism, and communism. In some ways, these movements spawn each other. They are all prophetic and religious phenomena—exposing perceived injustice and extolling a normative picture of humankind in the state of happiness. In evolutionary or revolutionary ways, each philosophy seeks to distribute and disseminate wealth.

The importance of Judaic roots in my own family and on the ethos of this nation has become clear these agonizing weeks as the amplitude of stupidities and sins behind the economic crisis surface. Millions of dollars of endowment funds have disappeared under the sleazy stewardship of Bernard Madoff from his "own faith community": Yeshiva University, Hadassah (Jewish Community Centers of North America), the Elie Wiesel Foundation for Humanity, and the like. Weren't we, at the very least, to look out for our own? And beyond that—so inferior ethic—what of the

Ten Commandments—"You shall not steal"? Rabbis and ethics teachers—most of us Jews and Christians—scurry back to the drawing board.

On the one hand, the constellation of values: individualism, freedom, private property, and deregulation characterize one perspective on sharing the wealth. These impulses lead more in the direction of *laissez-faire* philosophy and economics. On the other hand, we have the essential constellation of values: solidarity, justice, sharing, deontological (including legal) constraints on private action, progressive tax policies, and the like. The U.S. and Great Britain, and their impressive entourage in the global economy, world bank, and free trade communities serve as *avant gard* for this first heritage.

Economic systems flowing from the second way of life emphasize social formats such as communitarianism, socialism, and Marxism. Systems reflective of this orientation are found in Cuba, China, to a lesser extent Russia and Eastern and Western Europe, and Hispanic America. This communitarian focus also predominates in the Islamic world, although with great variation.

Though human freedom and liberty of action is on rapid ascent around the world and most new nations aspire toward some sort of republic or democracy, the constituting public policies derivative of this worldview remain controversial—especially free enterprise, non-regulation of commerce and markets, restricted national governments, and burgeoning sectors of law, business, and finance. Each philosophical and policy accent brings certain advantages and down-sides. Here is just one example of disadvantage from each school of thought.

Protecting the Wealth

"Protecting the wealth" seems to propel the world, at least in its present presentation, toward greater distance and disparity between rich and poor. In Samuelson's charts and tables in *The Great Inflation* and in Nobel Laureate Paul Krugman's *The Return of Depression Economics*,[27] we are evidently racing into a world where the gap between the top one-fifth and bottom one-fifth become a fast-widening chasm. In this disparity, Marx would find inevitable discontent, envy, and revolution.[28]

---

27. See Krugman, *The Return of Depression Economics.*
28. See Samuelson, *The Great Inflation.*

Spreading the Wealth

"Spreading the wealth" seems to stifle initiative. If we equalize or standardize, people will we be able to hire the best minds to be CEOs of corporations whose package of compensations, perks, and parachutes are curtailed? What shall happen to the New York Yankees—today whose payroll stands at double that of the next team in line— the poor Boston Red Sox,—an action defended as "public service" today by the home-town *New York Times*. And what of poor, struggling LeBron James when he becomes a free-agent next year? Will Wall Street team owners still be able to undergird a multi-year New York Knicks contract for him approaching half a billion clams? Hank Paulson's parachute from Lehman Brothers soared in those heights, yes, but not some kid from Cleveland.

The theological alternative I sketch in the next section of this essay seeks to mute the defects and dangers of these two economic schools of thought, even as I highlight the strengths of each as well. Freedom and justice, unrestraint and bounded-love synergetically united constitute human excellence—both personal and public. For now we must consider a most dangerous attitude toward our life in the world, one pertaining to our national purposes—economic, political, and military—and one having theological roots of wide currency—yet in error. This disposition I term a "Lust for Destruction."

ECOLOGY

Lust for Destruction

PRIDE AND LOFTINESS

I have in mind the generic disdain for the future and the apocalyptically exaggerated view of one's own importance and the importance of one's own people or religion. The phrase has engaged my mind since I first read it in Norman Mailer's *Of a Fire on the Moon*, an historical commentary on one of the early space adventures of NASA's Apollo program.[29] Interviewing religious persons along the Gulf Coast during those years, he found a recurring "middle-class lust for destruction." This posturing was at the same time an ascending to the clouds in an Apollo rocket for

---

29. See Mailer, *Of a Fire*.

a "Tower of Babel" vista—"all the Kingdoms of the world, I will give into your hand" (Matt 4.8 ff)—and a conscious or subliminal wish to watch it all come crashing down while you, left behind and unperturbed, watched on with glee.[30]

Gandhi speaks of the ominous quality of observing differing sorts of destruction, even those of a more subtle and self-deluded nature:

> An armed conflict between nations horrifies us. But the economic war is no better than armed conflict. This is like a surgical operation. An economic war is prolonged torture. The movement against war is sound. I pray for its success. But I cannot help the gnawing fear that the movement will fail if it does not touch the root of all evil—human greed.[31]

St. Augustine found the horror of all violence and war as the threat of losing peace and the security of home, hearth, and church to "out-of-control" unpredictabilities as frightful as disease and capricious accidents or attacks from enemies craving only to rape, pillage, destroy freedom, and unsettle. The God called on in such exigency is the God who reinstates peace and tranquility. God alone can and will spare His faithful people from insidious assault of every sort for Christ's Namesake. Travail may ensue in the meanwhile of the City of Man until the judgment of righteousness gives over the victory to *Civitas Dei*.[32]

Like all lusts, the lust for destruction is *Superbia* (pride), which shouts in the face of the good and great God demanding that we know a better will and way than God's will and way. While we extol our ways of harm and Holocaust, God's *Magnificat* way—standing over against our loftiness—is the breaking down of the mighty in order to lift up the lowly: "*Parcere subjectis et debellare superbos*" ("to spare the conquered and bring down the haughty").[33]

30. See Vaux, *Subduing the Cosmos*.

31. See Gandhi, "Non-violence."

32. Augustine, *The City of God*, Book 1, chapter 1.

33. Virgil, *The Aeneid, Book* VI, 854.

Tribulation

INTERPRETATIONS OF TRIBULATION THEOLOGY

Tribulation consciousness, both as treacherous fantasy and authentic righteousness, is another attitudinal valence that comes into play as we assess the theological adequacy of the religious worldviews that affect our nation's postures and programs in the world. Biblically speaking, "tribulation" confronts us in the trials that inevitably cross our paths of day-to-day living—loss of loved ones, accidents, job losses, etc. (Deut 4.30). It also refers to temptational experiences accompanying some cataclysmic event: ". . . then there shall be great tribulation" (Matt 24.21). The latter kind of tribulation—which has never occurred before and will never again occur—is a call to relational faithfulness with God and to relational righteousness with the neighbor and the world. Tribulation can also be a cop-out and opt-out. Theological and ethical righteousness rises in the first two modes. The latter mode is found in the defective theologies I seek to illumine in this part of the study.

Tribulation as cop-out and opt-out is found in the innumerable theologies that arise in dispensational and apocalyptic religiosities. It is usually associated with end-of-the-world scenarios that inspire the faithful to "wait for," "hope for," and most insidiously, "work for." This kind of tribulation consciousness creates a dangerous lack of responsibility, the kind that both causes and expresses the worldwide crisis of the war on terrorism and the global economic crisis of 2008.

We are meant to wait on God, to believe in Messianic coming and coming again, to believe and act according to expected justice and judgment as if we were responsible now and at the end. We are meant to live proleptically—as if God really were active in the world bringing and working about His redemptive will. If we live and act as if "God with us" does not exist, then we are, as Pope Benedict suggests, tearing down the world around us. In responsible tribulation, we live to honor God and creation.

At this point, when I am teaching a course on "Theology and the World," I will take the class into an interfaith scriptural reading on the subject of biblical tribulation within the events of world history. In a study where Jews, Christians, and Muslims work together, we consult textual chains from all three faiths—such as Ezekiel 38, Revelation 20, and Surah

23 (the Prophets). While cross-scriptural research has not yet advanced to the point where we know the exact *midrashic* lines of influence across the three Holy writings, one can sense their clear resonance.

Tribulation is a cognate phenomenon in the three Abrahamic scriptures. An actual historical oppressor holds the faithful community under attack, especially by reason of their confession and way of life. In secular coinage, an individual, group, or people take a stand against prevalent idolatry or injustice and call for repentance and ammendation of life. This threatens the dominant power into castigation and attack. The oppressor or "antichrist" demands apostasy, idolatry, and immorality—allegiance to its purported divinity. The ensuing persecution and martyrdom follows decalogic and *Akedic* patterns—where observance of the faith and life and the witness which is thereby entailed takes one into the realm of suffering, death, and resurrection. In this understanding, tribulation becomes liberating and saving, but it is hardly exclusive to the religious community.

The relevance of the concept for my cache of issues—empire, economic deprivation and collapse, militarism, and America's place in the world—hinges on the issue of who has done what wrong. Was the invasion and occupation of Iraq licit or unjust? Was the economic collapse caused or precipitated by some nation, some class of business people, some school of economic thought—philosophy and ethics? If my thesis is correct that the economic crisis, in large part, can be attributed to our exploitation of the poor, then how does this injustice play into the phenomenon of tribulation?

For example, those nations being hit hardest by the economic collapse are the bottom 30 on the poverty scale—all African nations and all classified by the Western affluent "category setters" as potentially failed states. How do we theologically and ethically evaluate this historical development? As we say in theology (but refuse to believe or act on), if God has a "preferential option" to the poor or is on the side of the oppressed, what is the theological meaning of the fiasco of Wall Street? The explosive trigger of the housing bubble? The American occupation and mass killing of civilians in Iraq and Afghanistan? Israel doing the same in Palestine and Gaza? What of the hegemonic placement of bases around the world, starting in the middle East and Africa? Tribulation is often thought to be an "act of God" or a "natural law"—the way we used to understand "famine" before Nobel Laureate economist Amartya Sen revealed the human etiology.[34]

---

34. See Sen, *Poverty and Famine.*

The End of the World

FAITH, LOVE AND THE KINGDOM OF GOD

In the deep midwinter, the world waits in silent yearning. At the end of winter, we enter into Lent, Ash Wednesday, and the mystery of the sheep's horn in Abraham's sacrifice—and the sacrifice of that other paradigmatic *monogenes, agapetos* ("only begotten, beloved son," Septuagint).

The ram's horn becomes the call for renewal, New Year's, and Jubilee. Even historical crisis, natural calamity, and cosmic death become *Akedic* mystery of death and God's new creation. No "flesh and blood cannot inherit the Kingdom of God" but "this mortal must put on immortality" (1 Cor 15). This world was not a mistake, but the beloved creature of God. So we trust its present resolution and ultimate finality to that love.

The world passes away. Economy and ecology are transient envelopes. Yet we know if this house (*oikos*) be destroyed, we have another intransient and indestructible (2 Cor 5.1). Christians, like Jews and Muslims, end the season of prayer with the phrase "One God, world without end, Amen." What a bold assertion. We may now see the reason for the strange admixture of topics offered in this section of my argument. We also may see now that the final parameter (one that is largely subliminal)—the end of the world—may ultimately shape the way persons and peoples believe and act. Faith and hope are assertions of love and the future against a hopeless world. It is the irresistible correlate of "one God." Attitudes like *Après moi, le déluge* or the lust for destruction disclose the failure of faith and love. Politically speaking, hate seeks destruction, while hope seeks peace. If perpetual peace is the antidote and antithesis of permanent war, the kingdom of God is the inversion of the end of the world.[35]

In kingdom purview, Luther and countless others retort, when asked what they would do if they found the world was coming to an end, say "I would plant a tree." Yet, in a strange paradox, as Kierkegaard would remind us, while the kingdom may be thought of as the earthly fulfillment of all things, in a Pauline sense, forsaking or relinquishing all may be the precondition for God to be "all in all," the end of "all as we know it." Still it is not for us to know or bring about the end of the world. The young brother of the Welsh family in John Ford's "How Green Was My Valley," who became disabled in saving his mother when she fell through the ice,

---

35. See Vaux, "The Rules of War," (available from ken-vaux@garrett.edu).

says to the pastor, "Yes sir, when Spring comes and the flowers bloom, I'll walk again." And as Sister Helen Prejean claims in *Dead Man Walking,* "Execution is the opposite of baptism."[36]

In this essay, I have confronted the crisis and end of one political, military, and economic era and the beginning of the new. It has been an era of extensive and deep crisis for America's role in God's world. Ultimately, as we will see in the next section exploring the theology of H. Richard Niebuhr, it is God, not us, who rules and controls the world.

CATASTROPHIC ENDING OR NEW BEGINNING

The end of the world becomes a deep-grained metaphor in such a period of crisis and hoped-for renewal. In *The End of the World and the Ends of God,* John Polkinghorne, my colleague at Cambridge, summarizes a grand project in which scientists and theologians grappled together with this provocative topic common to both disciplines.[37] The end of the whole universe as we have come to know it seems inevitable through one of many scenarios. Though cosmic beginnings can now be accurately studied through the "tracers" coming from the "Big Bang," cosmic endings are less certain and must be extrapolated from various trends now in motion. The trends, summarizes Polkinghorne, agreeing with his Cambridge mathematician colleague of the last generation, Bertrand Russell, is that "the world is destined to extinction in the vast death of the solar system" and that we have an impressively fine-tuned and fruitful universe which is condemned to ultimate futility.[38] These are strong words, especially as they suggest a derivation from the Epistle to the Romans where the Apostle claims that this world "is subjected to futility, not by its own necessity but by the will of Him who subjected it in hope" (Rom 8.20 ff). Though rejecting his "atheistic physicalism," Polkinghorne finds validity in the words of Steven Weinberg: "The more the universe seems comprehensible, the more it seems pointless."[39] One widely held representative scenario holds that the ever-expanding universe we now inhabit will eventually dissipate into a sterile collocation of weakly interacting molecules at a low level energy background where "cosmological heat death will occur, and the

36. Prejean, *Dead Man Walking,* 108.

37. See Polkinghorne, *The End of the World.*

38. Polkinghorne, *The End of the World,* 120–21 and Burtt, *The Metaphysical Foundations,* 23.

39. See Weinberg, *The First Three Minutes.*

universe will cease to sustain life of any kind."[40] Gravity and entropy will eventually pull back the expanding universe in a contracted fiery melting pot of matter and energy. Alternatively, the dark energy that constitutes 70 percent of the universe—Einstein's "cosmological constant"—may cause the universe to become unglued with the "big rip," and all will fly apart into oblivion. Just as that other fine-tuned organism—the living man—grows old and wears out, all human systems and sciences will pass away. Though the burn-out may occur next year or one trillion years from now, it will happen.

Economics, politics, and military exploits—though far reaching in the good and evil they bring about—are ultimately tiny blips on the screen of worldly significance. The broader patterns of justice and peace and the sustaining force precipitating such goods—and allowing contradictory evils—are divine patterns and ways that "sway the future."

Polkinghorne gives little credence to the "negentropy" proposals— such as a refinement of information concentration so great as to offset the seemingly inevitable degradation or the *deus ex machina*, God-of-the-gaps emergence within the possibilities of Heisenberg's uncertainty principle—that some alternate universe will emerge as quantum fluctuations flow out of a vacuum is highly probable.

Scenarios entailing human irresponsibility accompany these Noachic saving proposals. Thermonuclear, hydrogen, and far advanced chain-reaction calamities might bring an end to all life through our "warring madness." Famine, hunger, and global inhabitability may starve and choke all life. Humanly contrived biological and chemical processes also may infiltrate the natural processes and cycles knocking them into oblivion. Mighty nations seeming like Gog and Magog may appear to threaten all of what Teilhard de Chardin calls the achievement of "humanization in the cosmos."[41] Calamity may rush along ecological or economic pathways, given the frantic pace of our exploitation of the world. On present course in, say 1,000 years, humans will have extracted and exhausted the fuel hydrocarbons—oil, coal, gas, wood—so that earth can only sustain a small portion of its present carrying capacity. Even with enormous advances in energy production, as the Club of Rome showed in the 1960s, forces such

40. Polkinghorne, *The End of the World*, 27.

41. Pierre Teilhard de Chardin suggests that humanity and the cosmos are becoming progressively more "humanized," evolving toward greater human character and increased unity and harmony. See Teilhard de Chardin, *The Phenomenon of Man*.

as severe depopulation, disease, war, and hunger might advance to force the earth into precipitous eco-human collapse.

Again, we find here a horrific scenario. Global warming, species extinction, and other human failures such as economic greed and lack of stewardship have become ominous only in the last few seconds of geological time. Human-error or malice scenarios, for the most part, are sub-cosmic. The grandeur of the cosmos can absorb these mistakes, correct, and compensate. Only acts of God or inherent cosmic disintegration have the power to conclude creation as we know it. Coming in consummation is only in God's good time.

It is important at this point to affirm that human freedom and responsibility, care and disregard, hope and hate—do matter. Paul Ricoeur has shown clearly that human mythic construals—both cosmogenic and "cosmothanic"—arise in our science, economics, and conscience with preserving or destroying effect. Our symbolism of good and evil form both theodicy and anthropodicy—the "why" responses that change the world and the questions that haunt us: What can I do?

Seeing the connectedness with the Other and with all others makes it so. Polkinghorne affirms such theological seriousness. After dismissing the sad array of theological projections of the end which he finds as illusory, self-adulating, or unduly optimistic, he picks up the ancient philosophical arguments for life-ever-after from the incompletion and terrible injustice of what now goes on in the cosmos. "We shall all die with unfinished business and incompleteness in our lives. There must be more to hope for."[42]

Though I have always found this argument less than convincing, Polkinghorne does turn to the substance of his argument, which is that the Trinitarian God and the resurrection of Christ—the ultimate vindication and victory of Abrahamic messianic redemption—holds within itself the mystery of the end of the world. Building on the experienced excellence and provision of the world, in its "deep order" and "the fruitfulness of its history," the resurrection illumines those intimations of providence through all eternity.[43]

The theme of forgiveness now becomes central in the contention that the story of God with humanity and creation will go on. The injection of

42. Polkinghorne, *The God of Hope*, 99.
43. Ibid, 139.

this point at this moment is somewhat disturbing. Not only is the redemptive content missing, but also his account seems to imply that the universe will "come apart," and creation will be refuted because of the wrongs of humanity. In terms of the complicated interconnections of this essay, Polkinghorne's view is problematic. If God's will is thwarted because of human sin or if some evil can be imputed to humanity by which we must now assert (and assist?) the end of the world, the logic is perverted. To blame the world's end on human transgression or to take matters into one's own hands to save the earth—not in a Gilgamesh quest or a messianic visitation, but in a great act of vindication or retribution—seems to be the primal sin C.S. Lewis ponders in *Perelandra* or the *That Hideous Strength*.[44]

The great strength of Polkinghorne's analysis is the way he joins the cosmic and the existential in a single rich eschatology of God, people, and the world. That we humans experience decay and death is not only mimesis (Ricoeur) of the cosmos, it is the clue to the exasperating enigma and exuberant eschatology of human experience. It also associates ethics or the goodness of God with the vast dramatic process of cosmic evolution and devolution which otherwise becomes impersonal and grotesquely absurd.

In one of the essays of Polkinghorne's project, Princeton Seminary New Testament Professor Donald Juel (who tragically died at the conclusion of the eschatology project), writes on the death, fascination, denial, and transfiguration of the Gospel of Mark. As Juel has shown in his *Akedic* renditions of the messianic passages in the Gospels, particularly Mark, he now ponders with the aid of Ernest Becker.[45] Mark's confrontation of Jesus with death can be seen in the premonitions, warnings, rigorous castigations (Peter), and ultimately his thoroughgoing teaching that this is what it is all about—even the history and end of the world. The finality of death in Mark excludes any romantic or docetic denial of its reality, but squarely faces its inevitability, horrendous finality, and then gracious efficacy as the way "it has to be" and was "meant to be" all along. Now we find Jonas' "blessing of mortality" and Derrida's *Donner la Mort*.[46]

As I noted earlier, the threat and possible thrill of being present for—even "bringing on" war, economic nightmare, and ecological conflagration—is part of the apocalyptic impulse. That I was prepared

44. See Lewis, *Perelandra and That Hideous Strength*.

45. See Polkinghorne, *The End of the World*, 171–83 and Becker, *The Denial of Death*, xvii.

46. See Jonas, "The Burden and Blessing" and Derrida, The *Gift of Death*.

for and delivered to "a time such as this" is part of the inspiration and propaganda of all war scenarios: Think of the great text/film moments such as Agincourt or the Landing at Normandy beaches. "Only I can superintend the end," it is audaciously supposed. The eschatology essays in Polkinghorne, though addressed to cosmological rather than military or economic matters, illustrate the relevance of this present matrix of themes for the concerns addressed in this essay. Juel's somber and solemn evaluation from Mark is in the heart of Prophetic, Wisdom, Jesus, Pauline, Augustinian, and Islamic sanguine sobriety about war, the bewilderment of economic deprivation, and the necessity for peace.

The passage I would set beside Mark, with his repeated false starts and stops, is an equally early evangelistic text of the Apostle Paul. This text, revealing Paul's penchant, fills in the details of theology and theodicy that Mark intends and rounds out our picture of a theology of death in and of the universe:

> For God, who commanded the light to shine out of darkness, hath shined in our hearts, to give the light of the knowledge of the glory of God in the face of Jesus Christ. But we have this treasure in earthen vessels, that the excellency of the power may be of God, and not of us. We are troubled on every side, yet not distressed; we are perplexed but not in despair; Persecuted, but not forsaken; cast down, but not destroyed; Always bearing about in the body the dying of the Lord Jesus, that the life also of Jesus might be made manifest in our body. For we which live are always delivered unto death for Jesus' sake, that the life also of Jesus might be made manifest in our mortal flesh. So then death worketh in us, but life in you. (2 Cor 4.6–12)

Like Paul's Letter to the Romans—especially Chapter 8—we find here in Corinthians, cosmic reflections for the doctrine of Jesus as *Christos*. As a body conveys cosmic meanings, Jesus as Christ links humanity (the world) with divinity (God). What transpires (necessitates and culminates) in His death is a participatory parable about the death of the world. Paul's thesis is that, for there to be Christic/Messianic life (Resurrection), there must be death. The Apostle and the disciple are in the passage to life through death—so with humanity and the world. Only as death comes can life arise. As Karl Rahner says "Hope is a matter of letting one's self go."[47]

---

47. Rahner, "On the Theology of Hope," 235.

As in the world in its penultimate process (geological, biological, and sociological), from the decay and dissolution of one generation comes the vitality of another. As with the world when persons are battered and broken down, new life is being made ready. As the song goes "...and when I die and when I'm gone, there'll be one child born in this world to carry on."[48] Indeed, that particular waning, or perhaps culminating, life or world is being made ready for its own full and real life through the assault it endures. The radical biblical thesis offered here goes beyond Polkinghorne's strong eschatology by contending that not only does God's love and providence ultimately hold sway as the world deteriorates and passes into oblivion, but that in that *Akedic* mystery, the ashes of death are aroused into life.

CONCLUSION

I have surveyed a range of attitudes and dispositions that lead to a set of deficient theologies (heresies that are almost true), which, in turn, contribute to the global crises involving America and its role in world affairs outlined in Part One. I now turn to constructive theological proposals that will make possible a turn-around at the pragmatic level, providing a chance for a new direction for our nation in God's world today.

---

48. Laura Nyro, "And When I Die," *Stoned Soul Picnic: The Best of Laura Nyro*, Legacy, 1997 (compact disc).

3

Creative Theology
and the Promise of a Better Future

SECURITY

A Theology of Nations

THE NIEBUHR BROTHERS

A S WE PONDER THE issue of America in God's World, we find a most
comprehensive and insightful theology in the comparative work of
the Niebuhr brothers: Reinhold (1892–1971) and H. Richard (1894–1962).
Though their work comes at mid-twentieth century—a time of ominous
enemies in the world and a time of unprecedented opportunity—their
corpus is the most satisfying theological treatment we have of the history,
politics, and economics of America's role in God's world.

Reared in the parsonage of a German Evangelical Pastor in the
Midwest, both brothers (along with their sister Hulda, a theologian in her
own right) honed their ethical discernments during the global economic
crisis of the 1920s. Reinhold's studies—*Moral Man in Immoral Society*, *The
Nature and Destiny of Man* and *An Interpretation of Christian Ethics*—reflected his theological journey from socialism to liberalism and his heartfelt
desire to be seen as a patriotic American, shaking off his German roots.[1] H.
Richard was a serious scholar of the German tradition—Karl Barth and the
earlier generation that included Friedrich Schleiermacher, Ernst Troeltsch,
Max Weber, and others. Among many works, he wrote *The Social Sources of
Denominationalism*, *Christ and Culture*, and *The Responsible Self*.[2]

---

1. See Reinhold Niebuhr, *Moral Man*; *Nature and Destiny*, and *An Interpretation of
Christian Ethics*.

2. See H. Richard Niebuhr, *The Social Sources*, *Christ and Culture*, and *The Responsible
Self*.

The contrast of the siblings' thought on America in God's World is scintillating and searching—a brilliant probe of the best theological thought this country has to offer. Reinhold offers a realist, deeply Reformed, and Augustinian anthropology and political theology. Here the doctrines of sin and aggression are clearly accented, along with a plea for national candor and repentance, to form a workable resistance to pride and evil in our own house and in the residences of our enemies.

The topic "theology of nations" deals with questions such as empire and exceptionalism, identity and destiny of nations, idolatry and injustice, philanthropy and reconciliation, war and peace, and theological unities and diversities within the community of nations. This discussion therefore calls on the wisdom of conservative and liberal theology.

Richard draws on the liberal and idealist traditions to search out the doctrines of reconciliation, passive resistance, and peace. In his view, God is not a warrior but a peacemaker. Because of the blissful concord allowed by the societal consensus of pre-interfaith, Protestant America, the brothers' dialogue also contains broad areas of agreement. This thoughtful, publicly-engaged encounter of theology, ethics, and society helped frame the lively national and international debates of the last 50 years.

In 1932, the brothers sharply disagreed on the issue of whether the U.S. should join battle against Japan on the occasion of its invasion of Manchuria. A set of theological and ethical issues gained sharp relief in this exchange. Richard begins the debate with an essay in the *Christian Century* entitled "The Grace of Doing Nothing."[3] He calls for "noninvolvement" and "repentance for our sins." This call has two meanings. On the one hand, it is like the Jews in Mainz as they are about to be torched to death by the Frankish crusaders in the eleventh century. They expressed repentance for their sins as they were about to die—but what had they done to bring about this atrocity? Today a thoughtful Jewish writer in *Haaretz* in Jerusalem calls the Israel bombing in Gaza as 2008 ends—killing more than 1,000 (mostly civilians)—lacking in wisdom but goes ever further to call it a "war crime." Such words are shocking then as now, unless there are mysteries of judgment and grace in God's allowance of such moments.

Secondly, Richard Niebuhr is aware of America's chicanery and vested interest in attacking the Japanese. Not only had we done much to bring about the crisis, but we stood by "licking our chops" at what we stood to

---

3. See H. Richard Niebuhr, "The Grace of Doing Nothing."

gain. Like Richard, Augustine was ever aware of the mixed causalities and eventualities on all sides in such historical tragedy. None was ethically pure and none exclusively guilty. "All have sinned and fallen short . . . " (Rom 3.23).

Richard's argument is based on his theology. God is working for justice and peace in the world. We should gently accept what "God is doing in the world," where all actions we face are God's good action for us and all humankind.[4] We should refrain from an audacious will that assumes that it is all "up to us." Hope, faith, and love—as opposed to desperate striking out and "taking matters into our own hands"—should be our posture.

Richard's is a theology of nations with a particular accent on the role of America in the unfolding of God's kingdom in world history. Since his work on the kingdom of God in America[5] and his Troeltsch/Weber interest on the sociological manifestations of religion, he is reflecting on the role of nations in theological history.

He first has documented how religion creates an atmosphere and ethos that animates what Tocqueville saw as the unique general piety and sensibility of Americans and the translation of this ethos into a broader public policy. God was working out his judgments in the events of nature and history, and there was little humans could do to alter those judgments.

His article has much of the same tone of *Gelassenheit* ("letting go/ surrender") we find in Abraham Lincoln's Second Inaugural, in which he scanned the rationale of slavery and the Civil War and admonished: "If every drop of blood spilled by the lash is requited by one spilled by the sword, we can only say that the Lord's judgments are good and righteous altogether"[6] Richard was convinced that Americans must shun the options of militantism, capitalism, and nationalism and search out what was required for the well-being of the entire human family on the good earth.

Full of *Rheinische Vernunft* (Kant's Pure Reason), Reinhold countered with "Must we do nothing?" in a later issue of the *Christian Century*. Cold and calculating, yet "full of passionate intensity," (W.B. Yeats), he chided his little brother for trying to solve irascible international problems with an ethic of "pure love." Justice, not love, applies to groups and nations. Hesitancy and withdrawal would only invite greater assertion and ag-

---

4. See H. Richard Niebuhr, *The Responsible Self*.

5. See H. Richard Niebuhr, *The Kingdom of God*.

6. Abraham Lincoln, Second Inaugural Address, March 4, 1865.

gression from those who would harm us. In themes that reverberated in the McCain/Obama campaign of 2008, sharp policy differences reflected razor-sharp theological distinctions.

As Reinhold had argued in *Moral Man and Immoral Society* that same year, coercion and vigorous action were required to restrain evil.[7] And still today, the verdict is out whether, for example, American and Israeli belligerence in the Middle East generates peace or further exacerbates resentment and violence. Reinhold's theology of history held that God's will was not benign and passive but active and sharp-edged, and the forces of nature and history were similarly rigorous, generating profound ambiguities within the dramas of human history. Enormous evil was potential, as were thrilling opportunities for good, justice, and peace. Mankind was sinful, and human endeavors and institutions were riddled with complex good and evil commingled. Reinhold once quipped when asked if the world was getting better or worse, "It is getting better and worse at the same time!" In the end, human history is tragic and Reinhold must side with his beloved Augustine, who finds the only lasting hope in the kingdom of God and the eternal city—the realm come down from and drawn up to heaven.

This paradoxical vision was debated in 2003 by British historian Niall Ferguson and Robert Kagan, founder of the neoconservative Project for a New American Century.[8] Ferguson found it remarkable that America continued to deny that it was an empire, even though its extension of power throughout the world continued to cut across military, political, and economic realms. Kagan denied that America was or sought to be an empire because it had no desire for colonies. According to Kagan, America did and should desire the extension of power and influence to enhance its own and global security, economic opportunity, and democratic commitments. The debate was a clear replica of that between the Niebuhr brothers 70 years earlier. Indeed the respective arguments of Ferguson and Kagan are drawn from the brothers both directly and through the eyes of many mediators, though they now have been stripped of their rich theological content. Still Ferguson's optimism and Kagan's pessimism reflect the Niebuhr mentors' just as surely as did the stump speeches of John McCain and Barack Obama.

7. See Reinhold Niebuhr, *Moral Man.*
8. See Ferguson, *Colossus* and Kagan, *The Return of History.*

In his biography, *Hard Call*, McCain sensitively invokes Reinhold to buttress his militant position on Iraq and the War on Terrorism. "The Paradox of War" is the chapter in which he claims—"Reinhold Niebuhr, the eminent American theologian . . . recognized the contradictions about the nature of war and man at war. The former pacifist who offered the most astute, eloquent, and persuasive denunciation of pacifism argued that, in essence, there are worse things than war (Augustine), and human beings have a moral responsibility to oppose those worse things, even by violence if necessary. A man who understood the paradoxes of war, he (Reinhold Niebuhr) urged us to fight with all our strength but without hatred."[9] McCain then quotes Niebuhr's 1942 essay in the *Christian Century*:

> To love our enemies cannot mean that we must connive with their injustice. It does mean that beyond all moral distinctions of history we must know ourselves one with our enemies not only in the bonds of common humanity but also in the bonds of common guilt by which humanity has become corrupted. The Christian faith must persuade us to be humble rather than self righteous in carrying out our historic tasks. It is this humility that is the source of pity and forgiveness.[10]

McCain found solace and support in Reinhold's thought into the fallibility and corruptibility within "the heart of man." He resists, however, applying the same propensity to error and corruption to his own nation whom he patriotically loves and for whom he is prepared to lay down his life. This sense of honor, to be sure, is willingness to lay down his life for his comrades in battle and his fellow countrymen back home in time of war—*e.g.*, Viet Nam:

> Selfish desire corrupts man in all his social pursuits no matter how well intended. Utopian schemes no less than the basest impulses of human beings, manifest the moral conceit, the original sin of pride, which makes an idol of our individual and collective goodness.[11]

Then candidate, now President Obama is also a protégé of Reinhold Niebuhr. This can be inferred from his wide reading at Columbia while a student there and by the strong influence of his Niebuhrian pastor, Jeremiah Wright. In an interview in 2007, Obama remarked to columnist

9. McCain and Salter, *Hard Call*, 320–21.

10. Reinhold Niebuhr, "Our Responsibilities in 1942."

11. McCain and Salter, *Hard Call*, 321.

David Brooks, that Reinhold Niebuhr was one of his favorite philosophers (though certainly not having the gravitas of George Bush's favorite).

Obama also noted that Reinhold refused to "herald America as the world's unquestioned savior." In an address to the national meeting of the United Church of Christ—the mother church of Trinity UCC—he noted the influence of Reinhold on problems facing the U.S.—including poverty, race, war, and unemployment—as "moral problems rooted in societal indifference, individual callousness, the imperfections of humans, the cruelties of man towards man, and the inescapable act of sin"—all stipulates of Niebuhr.

Obama further shows his indebtedness to Reinhold in a *New Republic* article:

> I take away (from Niebuhr) the compelling idea that there's serious evil in the world and hardship and pain. And we should be humble and modest in our belief we can eliminate those things. But we shouldn't use that as an excuse for cynicism and inaction. I take away the sense we have to make these efforts knowing they are hard and not swinging from naïve idealism to bitter realism.[12]

My own awareness and work for Obama leads me to believe that he is a realist in the tradition of one of Reinhold's mentors—Walter Rauschenbusch, in his claim that justice, love, and all goods are realizable, however imperfect in history.

David Brooks corroborates my view of Reinhold's influence on Obama in an essay in *The New York Times* entitled "Innocents Abroad." Quoting Obama in a 2008 Chicago speech, Brooks writes: "America must promote dignity across the world, not just democracy. It must lead the world in battling immediate evils and promoting the ultimate good." Further citing Obama speaking in Berlin, Brooks notes Niebuhrian tones:

- We must help Israelis and Palestinians unite.
- We must unite to prevent genocide in Darfur.
- We must unite so that Iran (and Israel?) will not develop nuclear weapons.
- The (Berlin and Israeli?) walls between races and tribes, natives and immigrants, Christians, Jews, and Muslims cannot stand.

---

12. E. J. Dionne, "Full Faith," *The New Republic*, March 20, 2008.

- These are walls we must tear down.[13]

Obama is clearly a pragmatist in the sense of the latter work of Reinhold.[14] My thesis and approach to political theology is found in a dialectic between Reinhold and Richard Niebuhr. From the retrospective of the early twenty-first century, we can see that a blend of realism and idealism, pragmatism and pacifism is now needed to reinvent America's posture for justice and peace, security and stability in a turbulent though profoundly and inescapably interdependent world.

CALL TO SACRIFICE AND SERVICE OR DESTRUCTION AND DEATH

Such a composite theology of life and death drawn from the dialectic forged by the Niebuhr brothers pertains to all theology of human existence. It holds that a crisis or *kairos* lies before each man and nation. In such crisis or interruption from *chronos*, "where all is made plain" (Prov 15.19), we reckon with God about our life and make Pascal's wager.

". . . Once to every man and nation comes the moment to decide, In the strife of Truth with Falsehood, for the good or evil side . . ."[15] This occasion of decision is called temptation or the "valley of the shadow." In the paradigmatic depiction of the people of Israel (or Buddha, Jesus, the Church, or Islam) the Mount of temptation or valley of the shadow is the moment where decision is made about how to live and die.

- Do we live or die to God or the self?

- Do we live or die to justice and for others or to violence and harm?

- Do we live reconciled to family, neighbor, even our enemies?

- Do we live in self-contempt, unforgiving guilt, and destruction or to grace and life?

Clint Eastwood's film *Gran Torino*[16] culminates his life-long and searching quest for these issues of meaning (ontology) of existence in God's world (If indeed, there is a God!). His masterpiece embraces all of these dimensions of *Why? What for? And where to?* (cf. Heidegger)

The film is set in the job-starved, refugee-inhabited (Hmong, Palestinian, and Southern slave descendents, etc.) Detroit of the early

13. David Brooks, "Innocents Abroad," *The New York Times*, July 25, 2008.

14. See Stone, *Reinhold Niebuhr*.

15. James Russell Lowell, "The Present Crisis," 1844.

16. *Gran Torino*, directed by Clint Eastwood, Warner Bros. Pictures, 2008.

twenty-first century. Eastwood portrays and directs the late-life story of Walter Kowalski, a veteran of Korea with an unbearable memory. He's one of the last white-ethnic residents in a Hmong and poor-black neighborhood. Drinking and smoking his already blood-expectorating lungs toward death in a frame house somewhere—it could be out along 100 Mile road—he struggles as a profane, bigoted widower to "try before I die, to make some sense of life."[17] Estranged from his neglected and petty sons and daughter-in-law, his saucy granddaughter tells him she craves his vintage 1972 Gran Torino—"when he dies."

The life/death moment rises when the two Hmong teen-agers next door, who have changed his bigoted heart and become his friends, are brutally bullied, raped, and intimidated to the point of shooting up their home. Walt and Thao contemplate revenge. The boy-priest, Father Janovich, who has confronted Walt's salvation destiny at the behest of his deceased wife ("He must come to confession"), shadows him to the gangster's home, but is forced by police to leave just before Walt's denouement—having made his terrible choice.

He confronts the four gang members as night falls in a *chiaroscuro-Rembrandt-like* profile—reminiscent of Eastwood's early westerns and his "Unforgiven." He reaches into his breast pocket and they riddle his already moribund body with AK-47s. As his deposed body exsanguinates in the dust, the hand falls from his breast-pocket with his Zippo lighter—an award for his service in Korea. As we glimpse the lighter, we see in the darkness that covers the earth the crystal sparkle of received confession and pardon of Walt's Cain/Abel crime in which he had shot and killed 13 boys—the last one in the face. The film ends as the gang is put away for life, Walt's white Lab Daisy is with Thao as they drive along Elysian green fields on Jefferson Avenue with his newly inherited Gran Torino, and Eastwood sings at his Jazz piano . . .

> So tenderly your story, nothing more than what you see, or what you've done,
>   Standing strong do you belong in your own skin?
>   Your world is nothing more than all the tiny things you've left behind.
>   A heart locked in a Gran Torino it beats a lovely rhythm all night long.[18]

17. "Candide" (Libretto), lyrics by Richard Wilbur, score by Leonard Bernstein, 1956.

18. "Gran Torino," lyrics by Jamie Cullum, composed by Kyle Eastwood and Michael Stevens, *Gran Torino*, 2008.

When one decides to live *en-theos* ("in God"), one is exposed to tribulation and bears the cross of lethal human animosity. Persecuted for righteousness sake, forsakenness may lead to danger—even to death. Deciding for God is to live for justice, non-revenge, and martyrdom. Christ—Messiah, Incarnation, Logos, Word—is the meaning of all for all. This redemptive complex is the righteousness of human existence—human frailty into true humanity—death into life.

Reinhold Niebuhr focuses his work on the existential and political drama of humanity—a true social philosopher; Richard focuses his work on the narrative of God within the travail of humanity in the world (cultural and spiritual), a true theologian. The synergy and complementarity of the two provides us with a workable constructive theology as we consider our place and America's place in God's world. As with Clint Eastwood, the personal and political intertwine in the reflection on the theology of the nation offered by the Niebuhrs. We summarize this topic through three themes from Stone's chapter "The U.S.'s Role in International Politics since WW II: National Interest, Power, and Imperialism."[19]

National Interest

National interest and security are mischievous themes about a felt necessity—both human and divine—for the country. They are ill-defined and abused notions, covering a multitude of sins. Reinhold's dialectical and paradoxical (cf. Kierkegaard/Barth) theology offers insight and direction as we seek an adequate theology of the national interest.

The "national interest" is an evolving and constantly changing notion. After the two world wars, it essentially meant vanquishing the "Axis" powers. Shortly after that allied victory, Churchill warned of an "Iron Curtain" separating Allied Russia from America, as communism displaced fascism as "evil empire" and whose Cold-War containment became the precondition of national interest and homeland security. Today the Iron Curtain and the Berlin wall have come down (though Israel's wall remains), and America's national interest has become a viable global economy dominated by the U.S. and resisting the threat of militant Islam. For the twenty years of the formative "New American Agenda," especially after September 11th anti-terrorism has been viewed as the key to protecting and projecting our national interest.

---

19. Stone, *Reinhold Niebuhr*, 168ff.

Underlying this hard-to-articulate formulation of national interest is a strong conviction that our nation has been entrusted with the bequest of freedom and democracy—a gift intended for the whole world. A cognate formulation concerns "a way of life." This is not our prosperity or morality, as questionable as these ambitions have become after *Abu Ghraib* and Wall Street. At the heart of our national vision of "who we are" is our generosity, our concern for the oppressed of the world, and our concerns for the "least of these"—be they the sick, women and children, or the suffering people of the world. This conviction about America's agenda in the world is very much like Albert Schweitzer's compassion—now exemplified by philanthropists like Bill Gates and Warren Buffett, the Peace Corps, or the compulsions of the turn-of-the-century missionaries in the ministries of teaching, health care, hunger alleviation, public health, and welfare for the poor.

The benign and praiseworthy side of national interest was counterbalanced by one more ominous, but nonetheless compelling: military and nuclear technology. The first priority of the populace, demanded of each political party in power as well as the constant undergirding "military-industrial complex," was that this nation maintain military, nuclear, industrial and, in some sense, economic superiority in the world. This ambition led not only a surreal sense of security, soon to be shattered by multiple terrorist acts epitomized by September 11th, but by untoward effects like "going it alone in the world" and an international arms race and trade that ruined the economies of most nations at least in their concerns for education, public health, and the broader social welfare. Following America's lead, even poor nations spend as much as 30 percent of their national budgets on security and defense (or is it offense?).

The Niebuhr brothers broke ranks on this matter, with Reinhold endorsing Cold-War hegemony, albeit with great caution, and with Richard (and his students, like former Princeton professor Paul Ramsey and University of Chicago professor James Gustafson) stressing the same realism, but giving strenuous attention to international justice, planetary awareness, peacemaking, and bioethics (equitable access to health care).

Again, a synergy and strength arose in the national and international theological/ethical community thanks to this debate. It slowly became clear that only theological ethics accenting freedom and accountability, national readiness and international controls, strength and solidarity, all undergirded by justice and love, would suffice in this new world.

POWER

A key category of theological analysis of the societal realm is that of power. All religion enjoins the reality of power in making its public presence. In Judaism, the One who brings the world into being and cohesion is mighty to the awe of his creation. Even earthly powers fall down in impotent recognition (Job 24.22). Jesus is full of *exousia*—an all embracing power manifest in miracle, nature control, and healing. To God's Messiah (empowered One) "all power in heaven and on earth is given" (Matt 28.18). In Christological creed, this phenomenon becomes "God, the Father almighty." *Allah Akbar*—that God is great and good is the profound power-center of Islam.

Reinhold uses this biblical impulse to inform his ambivalent description of human power. In sociological and philosophical categories, this becomes *yes, no, yes*—recognizable by its Augustinian tone. He celebrates the impulses of power that allow creative human action in the world. He warns against the disorienting and destructive power of pride. He honors and endorses the power that supplies cohesion and organization to human society even in the face of the fall and its disorder. This, even though creative power—endowed into human life through *imago Dei*—is always vulnerable to being twisted first to leading, then coercing, then subjugating others. Yet, its essence remains the genius and gift that makes existence—personal and corporeal—possible.

Reinhold further defines, justifies, and circumscribes military, political (ideological) economic, and religious (priestly) power.[20] An array of powers can be variously arranged and prioritized within the overarching purpose of balance and prudence—honoring God through serving the neighbor in justice, peace, and love.

> The spiritual and physical faculties of man are able, in their unity and interrelation, to create an endless variety of types and combinations of power, from that of pure reason to that of pure physical force.[21]

In our freedom and responsibility, we can make things better or worse in all these realms of power. The task of a useable theology is to develop criteria and principles to guide such critical and creative responsibility (*e.g.*, care of the earth, oneness of the human family, watching out for the most vulnerable, etc.). It should also remind society and the world

20. Stone, *Reinhold Niebuhr*, 177ff.
21. Reinhold Niebuhr, *Nature and Destiny*, 260.

of anthropological truths such as 1) human potentials for truth, justice, goodness, forgiveness, reconciliation, and peace; 2) human potentials for exploitation, deception, injustice, and violence; and 3) "the wisdom to know the difference." An example of concrete policies responsive to such theological imperatives would be rescuing and rehabilitating the vulnerable victims of Hurricane Katrina, the Iraq war, or the mortgage collapse.

Tough theoretical ethical work also must take place with theologians and secular experts on normative and descriptive analyses of concrete issues such as why, who, how, when, and where on matters like feeding the hungry, healing the sick, lifting the poor, protecting the aged and children, resisting the war-maker, and stopping the thief. All of these dimensions involve the use and abuse of power.

IMPERIALISM

Reinhold picks up on this theme of detailed, fine-grained analysis and action that is necessary when broad principles grounded in theology and philosophy are to be applied. In an article on the theology and ethics of crises in the Middle East (the Suez crisis) he writes: "The moral is that idealism is ineffective if it is not implemented in detailed policy. It is particularly dangerous when a great imperial power greater than that of Rome, namely, our own nation, is informed by such vague and fatuous idealism."[22]

As we enter the new year of 2009, the Middle East is in a period of acute crisis. The elected government of Gaza (called this morning "the militant Islamic rulers of Gaza," reminding us of 1 Macc 13.41), elected in premature elections insisted upon by the U.S. (perhaps animated by its "evil empire," Manichaean idealism), has declared that leadership "terrorist"(a Bush/Cheney designation). Gaza has apparently allowed or even undertaken the firing of thousands of rockets on Israel. Dozens have been killed, and there has been significant property damage. In the present Israeli counter-assault, devastating rocket attacks have taken out infrastructure, *Hamas* homes and buildings, and caused significant civilian death and injury.

In a recent interview with CNN, Zbigniew Brzezinski, the only recent State Department official to make some headway with Israel and the Palestinians in the Camp David accords and a protégé of Reinhold Niebuhr, offered such detailed analysis:

22. Reinhold Niebuhr, "The Situation in the Middle East," 43.

This has been going on for 40 years. There is no way that the present parties can resolve this. The U.S. must lead the way for the rest
of the world but the Bush administration has failed to provide such
leadership. The community of nations, The UN, and the religious
communities will follow such leadership. That coalition of parties
will be necessary for there to be a well planned, well implemented
peace settlement.[23]

Both Niebuhr brothers are supreme realists in the sense that they
insist that the full force of human will and heart, conscience and action
be marshaled to address a particular issue. Ideals and practices must intertwine in concerted approach. The widest spectrum of expertise and
persuasion must be considered. The widest circle of consensus must be
formed to be called on for support and implementation.

Another part of careful analysis refers back to our preceding discussion is the equation of power. Israel has determined since the Holocaust in
Europe that its people will never again be out-smarted and out-powered.
Israel will use its technology and its army of more than half a million soldiers,
will kill at a 100-to-one ratio if necessary, and go to a Masada-like death to
the last man, woman, and child to overwhelm any enemy. But is such determination potentially a demonic thing? Could there be some new David
with stone and slingshot ready to challenge this mighty Goliath? Former
Senate Majority Leader George Mitchell, recently named U.S. special envoy
to the Middle East, will seek to ameliorate the suffering and hostility in the
region and negotiate peace between the Israelis and the Palestinians. One of
the theological issues here involves two profound evils.

Shoah

First, there was the biblical event of *Shoah*, when Europe and the world
sought to exterminate people Israel from the face of the earth. Their resurrection was obtained only by the death camps and lethal refugee wandering (ship Exodus)—crying the *Kaddish*—and finding home only in
the new lands of Israel and America. Today Israel, America, and the world
community that yearns for peace on earth, good will to all people, hopes
for the peace and justice of Zion and *Haaretz* Israel.

---

23. Zbigniew Brzezinski, CNN interview, January 2, 2009.

Nakba

Second, there is the world's signature event of the late century and present, the *Nakba* ("catastrophe")—the cleansing of Palestinians, millions thrown into refugee wandering in camps and cages like Gaza—crying the *mezuzah*. They are sojourners on the face of the earth by act of the state of Israel, in concert with her only protector on earth, America.

Both of these social acts (evils) are or have overtones of being religious-genocides—Judaocide and Islamicide. No sins and evils on earth are more reprehensible—they are blasphemies to the God of creation and redemption.

The theological etiology of this *Akedah* (suffering/sacrifice) of the two sons of Abraham is located by Richard Horsley in his book, *In the Shadow of Empire: Reclaiming the Bible as a History of Faithful Resistance*.[24] Here he claims that Christianity (probably in concert with Judaism and Islam) cannot forcefully protest empire that is called for in scripture and certainly in Christ—because it now "is" empire.

These faiths of Abraham already have accommodated to culture—indeed they have themselves become empires or the handmaidens of empire in the search for power and security.[25]

> ... Christians are called to constitute alternative values, social relations, and to a degree an alternative society to the Roman imperial order ... The empire had indeed killed Jesus, but his crucifixion had become a symbol of opposition to the empire ... [26]

Perhaps only a transvaluation of values and a new resurrection morning can now save us from this dual crucifixion of God through His "beloved child" (Isa 53, John 3.16). The words of Yusuf Islam (formerly Cat Stevens) give us hope:

> Morning has broken, like the first morning ...
> Sweet the rain's new fall, sunlit from heaven,
> Like the first dew fall, on the first grass ...
> Praise with elation, praise every morning,
> God's recreation of the new day.[27]

24. See Horsley, *In the Shadow of Empire*.

25. See H. Richard Niebuhr, *Christ and Culture*.

26. David E. Anderson, "God and Empire," *Religion & Ethics Newsweekly*, October 31, 2008, Episode no. 1209.

27. Cat Stevens, "Morning Has Broken," lyrics by Eleanor Farjeon, *Gold*, A&M, 1995 (compact disc).

The Muslim's ballad is universal in resonance like Newton's "Amazing Grace."

ECONOMY

A Theology of Economics

Dialogue: Philosophy, Theology, and Economics

From Max Weber's *The Protestant Ethic and the Spirit of Capitalism*, R. H. Tawney's *Religion and the Rise of Capitalism* and Georg Simmel's *The Philosophy of Money*[28]—all written at the turn of the last century—we have witnessed a lively dialogue between philosophy, theology, and economics. That widespread interest of 100 years ago is echoed by a resurgence of interest today. At this troubled time of economic and political turmoil, such dialogue is imperative but highly difficult. The form, substance, and process of economics has become global, significantly virtual, intertwined with myriad cultural phenomenon, somewhat enigmatic, and hotly debated as to whether it is a positivistic, naturalistic, or normative activity. At the same time, philosophy and theology have changed profoundly as to their reach, definition, and relevance. Meaningful conversation resulting in cross-fertilization and reciprocal correction therefore comes hard even as it becomes more and more imperative.

I review in this short section of our essay three thinkers from the theological side, to help us develop a sketch of motifs promising fruitful dialogue: D. Stephen Long, the author of *Divine Economy* and a former colleague in Chicago, now teaches at Marquette University in Milwaukee. Kathryn Tanner, professor of theology at the University of Chicago, has written *Economy of Grace*. Douglas Meeks is professor of Divinity at Vanderbilt and the author of *God the Economist*. These thoughtful, critical, and constructive scholars have each done their homework on the new world of economics.[29]

---

28. See Tawney, *Religion and the Rise of Capitalism* and Simmel, *The Philosophy of Money*.

29. See Long, *Divine Economy*; Tanner, *Economy of Grace*; and Meeks, *God the Economist*.

ECONOMICS AND ETHICS

Steve Long begins his comprehensive study with a brief historical re-hearsal of the engagement of theology with economics. Taking off on the cursory sketch I have offered, he reviews the libertarian (J.S. Mill) and communitarian (K. Marx/ F. Engels) heritage and draws for his touch-points on Max Weber's analysis of the theoretical (philosophical) cor-relation of economics and ethics. Here Long also finds another critical, normative, and sometimes accommodating cultural *Geist* in the concrete faith traditions—Judaism, Islam, and the salient forms of Christianity: Catholic, Calvinist, Lutheran, and Wesleyan, in particular.

Long draws on this body of work to identify touchstones as we at-tempt to walk on uncharted water across the gulf separating the disci-plines of economics and theology. He finds three types of approaches to explore the connection. Each approach arises from a particular cache of values, proving the point that values determine what you see and how you describe phenomenon.

CAPITALIST ORTHODOXY

The philosophy of liberty (Mill) and theology of Calvin supply the con-ceptual apparatus to interpret and provide rationality for the empirical description of economic action from Adam Smith to Milton Friedman called capitalism. For Marx, the word becomes something of a pejorative (cf. *Das Kapital* and Simmel's *Philosophie des Geldes* with Adam Smith's *The Wealth of Nations*). From the outset, we see the inclinations, even at this early stage in the capitalist movement, of Anglo-American indi-vidualism and continental collectivism. Long places Michael Novak, Max Stackhouse, Dennis McCann, and Philip Wogamon as expositor-inter-preters of this line of thought called "capitalist orthodoxy."

Key doctrines coming both from Catholic and Protestant interpret-ers and representatives include freedom of invention and action, non-interference, and free expression of producer and consumer/maker and user interface, and free flow of one's earnings into private and public (pa-rochial) expenditure, savings, and philanthropy. One of Long's critiques of this school is its designation of capital commerce as possessing autonomy and near divinity. Constraining influence on the dynamic process should not come from church, crown, or even appointed or elected consistory. Hands off is called for on this Invisible Hand.

As I've heard across my professional career as an ethicist addressing businessmen, physicians, lawyers, even clergy: "Good 'men' will make good decisions." The mention of duty toward the community or any heteronomous normative doctrine draws quick and fiercely self-protective resistance. Milton Friedman was fond of saying that business had only three vectors of responsibility: owner's profits, labor's wages, and customer's prices. The only norms of ethics and spirit were those intrinsic to this three-fold interactional process. At this point we recall Chairman Greenspan's *mea culpa* that he was shocked that financiers "did not regulate themselves." The smile of the Cheshire cat remains even after the cat is gone. The haunting question now becomes that of "Cat" Stevens: Can economy survive the absence of the undergirding God and the fear of God—that manna in the fresh dew of morning—human responsibility?

Even Maynard Keynes' accession to "animal spirits" in economic activity is still a call to autonomy and inherent norms. Even this genius of community accountability remained a thoroughgoing capitalist. He refused to acknowledge any external designation of sanction—praise or blame—because it was superfluous. He, of course, did become the great advocate of public-policy *Steurung*—steering of the economy. This would even allow regulation and direct governmental stimulation—all in a new and surprisingly relevant version of liberalism.

One caveat is important in this sketch that might give the impression that immorality was rampant in "orthodox capitalism." Only later do we find what we now know as *Kapitalismus savage.* For example, for centuries, the fear of God (and congregational sanction) remained so strenuous that "economic sinners" could be called to the sinner's bench in Calvinist and Puritan churches. Those who overcharged interest on loans (or charged any interest on loans to the poor) or those who gouged customers (*e.g.*, cost of snow shovels in a blizzard) were called to the repentance bench as surely as sexual sinners. One wonders if Ken DeLay or Bernie Madoff faced the same stocks and were motivated to the same repentance.

Part one of *Divine Economy* explores J.S. Mill's salient development of ideas of liberty and their political, economic, and ethical import. Long also is interested in the influence of Thomistic philosophy on Mill's system. The influence of Aristotle, Augustine, and St. Thomas, of course, injects an element of moral theology into this philosophy of reason and its public manifestations. Of interest in my final reprise of a theology for the contemporary global crisis in Part Four also is the influence of Jewish and Muslim scholars on Aquinas. My theological interest on this point is not the "radical orthodox" commitments of Long and Milbank, but of contemporary impulses of interfaith understanding on economics and other issues.

Long also looks at the neo-Calvinist reading of conservative economics expressed by Princeton's Max Stackhouse, the neoconservative/Catholic view of Michael Novak and the Wesleyan/liberationist approach of Philip Wogaman. Long is critical of certain features of "orthodox capitalism." He also draws some elements from these thinkers into his synthesis in what he calls the "residual tradition." The "good" of "freedom of" belief, thought, expression, and action, as well as "freedom from" tyranny and coercion are among those elements.

Though a more Anglican and Hispanic thinker and constitutionally ill-disposed to Germanic (Hegel, Kant, Enlightenment), Long is meditating on Hegel's *Geist* or spirit as it pertains both to culture and religion. In a section on "Emergent" tradition, he affirms the social justice/care for the poor ethos of liberation thought, Catholic labor wisdom, corporeal and congregational bodies, even socialism.

Here alongside his customary mentors of evangelical-liberals is another circle of Long's heroes: liberationists Gutiérrez and Sobrino and two Garrett notables—Ruether and Cone. By visiting liberty as it is connected to original sin and co-creation and the development of these doctrines in Reinhold Niebuhr's realism, individualistic and ontological considerations are united with the structural and sociological. Creation, anthropology, axiology, and ecclesiology are doctrines that draw together the motifs of wealth and poverty, personal and public, church and corporation—within a more holistic theology and ethic.

In one of the best parts of his book, the one-time Methodist missionary in Latin America comes to terms with Marx adding prophesy and eschatology to his tool-kit. He transitions into his synthetic chapter, where he calls our attention to what he calls a "residual" school of thought. This is "radical orthodoxy," especially in its Milbank version—in its nascent formulation with Long. It is virtue theory,[30] shaped by the strange bedfellows, Hauerwas and McIntyre. The book's great value becomes apparent at this point. Here we have Long's penchant for metaphysics blended with biblical theology. His post-modern skills become clear, along with his helpful synthesis of Thomistic and Wesleyan/neo-orthodox theology.

---

30. See Hauerwas, *Vision and Virtue* and Vaux, *Powers That Make Us Human.*

We wait for further work from him reflecting his several dialogues with Kathryn Tanner, in which he has dealt with the profound crisis in economic life in the late decade. Here we also sense the "rub-off" effect of her skill at fine-grained economic analysis.

Divine Economy leaves us with several salient insights to apply to our analysis of the world's new and frightening economic crisis and the American role in the final section of this book:

- Capitalism is not a naturalistic or deterministic—a necessary phenomenon. It doesn't have ontological status or unquestionable ethical virtue. It is a compelling idea with a wide range of presentations over its very short history, but the life it has "on its own" may be divine or demonic. Long adopts Milbank's historical judgment that the epoch of thought and value in which capitalism arises—Spinoza, Hobbes, Adam Smith, and so forth—is dangerously materialistic and possessed with moral audacity.

- Similarly the anti-religious bias of the times is shown by Weber's "Iron Cage" where religion is dismissed as an irrelevant cultural factor and vital and influential theology is relegated to marginality—a superstitious relic. Rationalism within very narrow limits of justification invalidates much meaningful epistemology and axiology.[31]

- In the declarative last chapter we are left with the important prophetic idea that capitalism can be, as Milbank concludes, a heretical ontology of violence. We also welcome the related, proleptic (coming) idea that divine plenitude trumps scarcity in the Malthusian or Darwinian sense.

AN APPLIED THEOLOGY OF ECONOMICS

Kathryn Tanner followed Long's useful study by five years and Meeks' by 15 years. *Economy of Grace* offers not only an economic theology from the foundation of mainline Christian theology, but also one well-informed by careful dialogue with fellow University of Chicago scholars in economics and business. It therefore becomes an exemplary correlational or applied theology.

Her theology is personal, conversational, and pastoral. It is like the shocking theology reported by students of Dietrich Bonhoeffer and more recently of Henri Nouwen—real, living, personal—confronting you with

---

31. See Weber, *The Protestant Ethic.*

decisions about truth, God, justice, and who you must therefore become. This approach appeals to persons working in the world of business in the same way that sensitive biomedical theology appeals to workers, patients, and families in the fields of sickness, healing, life, and death.

What does the grace and love of God and violation and the communion of people say about money, sharing, and being poor? Her theology is deeply shaped by cultural anthropology and the very detailed and intimate behavioral analyses of political science. Her approach to economics becomes very relevant and helpful when people are losing their jobs, questioning their value, despairing at meeting payrolls as executives, or wondering how one can feed his family or send his children to college.

From this kind of pastoral approach, she broaches the theoretical and practical matters of economics: property, savings, investments, prices, taxes, helping others, welfare, foreign aid, alms, programs of development, and on and on. She poses a set of principles and action-imperatives that convey a program of theological conviction that inform my constructive proposals in Part Four.

THEOLOGY OF GRACE AND PLENITUDE, SIN AND RESPONSIBILITY

Tanner's theology of grace and plenitude, sin and responsibility can be summarized by the following taxonomy:

- God freely expends for others, so should we.
- God owns and gives, we receive and tend.
- Property is opportunity and temptation.
- God's being, activity, and proffered Way to us (Torah and Prophets) are a lot about money.
- The Trinity patterns, within humans and our communities, the divine givings and receivings.
- These givings and receivings constitute divine and human perfection.

Among the features of a theological economy we find: 1) economic interdependency; 2) actions benefit one and all; 3) those in need and helpless are favored; 4) transparency; 5) forgiveness; 6) unconditional giving; and 7) non-competitiveness.

The features of the theological economy ought to be embodied—as much as is possible—in our economy of capitalist exchange and in all other economies as they come and go (*e.g.*, Primitive Christian, Islamic, Jewish, Marxist, Socialist, etc.).

THE ECONOMY AND GOD

When I first read *God the Economist* some 20 years ago, I failed to realize what an innovative study it was. Don Shriver and Helmut Gollwitzer had written on rich and poor 20 years earlier.[32] Even earlier work by Joseph Fletcher and Andre Bieler had intrigued me.[33] But it was Doug Meeks who first opened up the cache of ideas of theology and economy to a broad American audience. This included the world of Church and corporation.

It may have been the good title. Just as the phrasing "God the physician" caught the imagination in early biotheology and ethics (Deut: "I am the Lord your Physician"), God the economist goes to the heart of the matter. Theological economics becomes requirement, not fancy, if God is the economist. Economy must be theologically perceived and conceived if God is the economist. If God has to do with economy, then economy must deal with God. Aquinas and Calvin, Adam Smith and Milton Friedman all knew this. They imperfectly, but so helpfully, moved toward formulating a synopsis and synthesis of God and economy. We can build on their heritage even amid the economic (and theological) cataclysm we are presently experiencing.

Meeks reminds us that theology as Church, *Umma* and Israel has always been about economics. God's work in heaven and on earth is what is connoted in the original word—economy. The "economy of God," a technical theological term, is still used to describe Trinitarian dynamics—the inner life of God as well as the broad environment of providence or the human world—God's work within the creation. From the Greek—*oikos*—we get "house" or "household" (inhabited world), "economy" and "ecology."

Not only is biblical material full of response to wealth and poverty, money, trust, fidelity, promise, debt, and redemption, it testifies that God is concerned with the substance and processes, the stuff and effects of economic reality. Meeks is solidly oriented in this biblical witness and draws his theology from this source.

God is involved in the minutia and details of the life and lives of each creature. "He opens His hand and satisfies the desires of every living thing" (Psa 145.16). Our times and the occasions of our existence—our

---

32. See Shriver, *Rich Man, Poor Man* and Gollwitzer, *The Rich Christians*.

33. See Fletcher, *Moral Responsibility* and Bieler, *The Social Humanism of Calvin*.

life and death, our well-being and sufferings—are in His hand (Psa 31.15). All the dimensions of life and existence—space and time, height and depth, in cosmos and in string-theory's strands, dark matter and the interstitial membranes where space and time collapse toward infinity and eternity—all are in His hands. God is and does beyond all that we can ask or think. In the vis-à-vis of economy, God guides the future as He has the past. He superintends calamity and opportunity—rendering all *chronos* spans—*kairos* moments. Crisis is just that—a fracture and fissure, occasion where all becomes new (Jer 31.22).

What are the central features of Doug Meeks' theology of economics? God is a property-owning economist in a sense radically different from the ancient world. The God of Israel, the Father of the Lord Jesus Christ (*kurios*, "owner" or "disposer," also is an economic word), and Allah ("*Ellah*," Aramaic was likely Jesus' name for God, along with "*Abba*"). Creation now is the household of God's distributed righteousness. This power of life and goodness over, indeed out of the *nihil* ("nothing")—is crafted by God in deliverance: creation, Exodus, healing and resurrection through His economist, humanity. The sermon I offered in October 2008 at the seminary where I teach elaborates the essence of this divine/human construction of the good economy of grace.

St. James Liturgy: Moral Finality in Mortal Flesh

Lectionary: Psalm 90, Matthew 22

I invite you to search with me today for that secret, "the pearl of great price." The burden of lectionary scriptures is God with and for us—*Deus Praesens, Christus Praesens*—that is the secret, the pearl, the Wisdom of God. If you are like Karl Barth, you wake each day—breathe in the *Ruach Elohim*, the *paracletos*—then settle to read the Bible in one hand and the newspaper in the other. When you do you may read these words.

"We must liquidate our toxic, illiquid assets and put the economy back on solid grounds." In the economic deluge of this autumn that has swamped all boats—where even the trickle down has dried up—perhaps such flowing jibberish from lawyers, even clerics—may be forgiven.

In our Gospel lection, one such corporate lawyer approached that Rabbi *par excellence*. He brought a life-or-death question disguised as a philosophical conundrum (you know the kind of questions we all ask, "Doctor . . . I have this friend . . ."): "Tell me Master, what is the greatest of all principles?" (Mt 22.35)

The answer you know well: Love God with all your being and love your neighbor as yourself. That's the bedrock under all the floods of the world-springs of life.

The same all-on-the-line Q and A recalls a dialogue with another attorney: "What must I do to be saved?" (Lk 10.25 ff) And the answer was the same—all or nothing. "You belong to God and the neighbor—that's the prime mandate." Then point seven in the sacred tableau: "Don't steal and what you have—share with the poor." Both legal men looked for escape and shelter: ". . . But who is my neighbor? . . . Surely, I can't give up everything I have?"

Confronted by the sacred heart, they could not join their heart to His . . . and both walked away . . . with great sadness.

Our Hebrew lectionary probes this underlying wisdom, the Tao of all creation, embedded within these Christ encounters. Psalm 90 speaks that quintessential wisdom to my life. After months of health crisis, I treasure the words: "Lord you have been our dwelling place in all generations. Before the mountains were brought forth or ever you had formed the earth and the world—from everlasting to everlasting—you are God! You turn men to destruction . . . as you give construction, you are the giver of birth and life—suffering and death— a near and dear intimate in all that transpires." This is the theological key to all theodicy and providence.

All flesh is grass—and then that uncanny indicator of our human life span across this 5,000-year interglacial age—three score and 10 and if, by reason of strength, of four score, still toil and sorrow—and we fly away. So teach us to number our days and apply our hearts to wisdom.

As part of my quest to meet God in the morning, I often walk the streets of town as the curtain of night lifts for the new day. One grey dawn this summer, I watched two silver coyotes streak down Ashland avenue on their way to the next woodlands. As space and time fly by before us like streaking wild creatures at dawn, the psalm sees a curtain splitting time and eternity—here and there—like a ghost town or field of dreams. Here we learn the Dives/Lazarus lesson. The incredible gift and grace of life is given here and now from there and then. Our task and the Lord's Prayer seek to bring that kingdom on earth as it is in heaven.

With Garrett Professor Julie Duncan's help I've become aware of *Koheleth*—Ecclesiastes—these reflective days. With the wanderer Gilgamesh, searching for wisdom, I count as precious the "one who lies in my bosom and the tiny hand resting in mine." I cherish the three new grandchildren come out to us these *kairos* months.

This biblical kernel has led me for many years to consult Jewish and Muslim wisdom as corroboration for the meaning of scripture. Our three Abrahamic scriptures are *midrashic* continua or chains. Following a path from Hebrew to Christian and Muslim insight yields the following truth about God and life.

This sermon is an example of interfaith biblical reasoning. Judaism leads the Abrahamic faith family into what Muslim leaders, in the most important religious document of our time calls "A Common Word." Its essence is the call to the "love of God and neighbor." Hebrew texts formulate these synergic two loves as a "redemptive complex" that Christianity and Islam take up in turn. This quintessence of faith and life is spoken of as a sprout that springs up in the desert of the world. The composite Abrahamic tradition tells of God's healing messianic gift to the world and our responsive act of doing justice and care. In this way the synergy— the Sophia of "loving God and neighbor"—is activated.

The complex can be seen as divine indicative yielding human imperative:

The hungry are fed . . .
  Thirsty are given drink . . .
    Homeless sheltered . . .
      Sick healed . . .
        Blind see . . .
          Lame walk . . .
            Possessed exorcized . . .
            Prisoners released . . .
            Oppressed liberated . . .
            Poor encouraged . . .
            "Least of these" honored . . .
            Sinners forgiven . . .
            And the dead are raised . . .

A cornucopia of grace. Jesus claim to the lawyers is that God's righteousness—what Walter Brueggemann calls God's godness—is our faith/work. *Gabe* and *Aufgabe*—gift as task. God's proleptic action becomes our present assignment. "I am doing a new thing—do you perceive it?" And Jesus' words become awesome and wonderful: "The works I do . . . you will do greater for I go to the Father" (John 14.12).

You will recognize this complex of redemption . . .
. . . from the pre-biblical Egyptian Book of the Dead

... Hebrew *Tanakh* (Torah, prophets and writings)
... and Jesus inaugural commentary at Capernaum based on
Isaiah 61 and his last judgment scenario in Matthew 25.

On King Tut's tomb is text from ancient Pharonic Egypt where
at judgment our heart is weighed for righteousness on the scales
of justice. "Did you feed the hungry, clothe the naked, shelter the
exposed?"

"If your heart keeps right," as the old Sunday-school ballad goes,
"there are songs of gladness in the darkest night."
"Well done, good and faithful servant" is the verdict and one circles
the underworld into the everlasting light of the cosmos.

All wisdom from the ancient near east, India, the Orient and
Africa sings the same song. Righteousness is entailed in salvation;
love of God of necessity entails love of neighbor; business, even war,
entails ethics. There is no morally neutral zone in this world—all
counts and is accountable. The American myth that certain realms
like science and economics are autonomous and morally neutral is
untrue and dangerous. Remember the wisdom of Proverbs (11.1):
"tipping the scales is an abomination to the Lord." Evangelism
and ethics are one. Faith and justice converge. At the throne of
God—righteousness and mercy shall kiss (Psalm 89).

Surely, we must stand in fear and trembling, as in the liturgy of
St. James of Jerusalem, we sing as mortal flesh is silent before moral finality. As in the letter of Jesus' brother, echoing Psalm 90, the
downtrodden should rejoice as they are raised up and the rich as
they are brought down, for as the flower of the field they shall pass
away, and when we pass away we must be ready to flow through
the membrane of space/time to the bosom of Abraham. There the
rich Jew, Christian, and Muslim will pass the curtain to the poor
Lazarus. Right now the mighty in this country and the privileged
world are being cast down. Our nation, to which so much has been
given and from whom so much will be required, has visited God's
world with war and torture, greed, and exploitation, and now in
judgment we are being brought low. But in divine purview that
may be a gift. I believe we are being called from assertion and aggression to sharing and service, justice and love—life-giving rather
than death-dealing. Perhaps, as the rich Dives we are to be given a
glimpse of the poor Lazarus, and another chance—then as those
rich lawyers we might receive the great turnaround of forgiveness
and instead of walking away in sorrow like the Prodigal we will
run home in joy.

The gem we contemplate buying with "all that we have" sparkles
like an African diamond cut in Antwerp. It is replete in Hebrew

history. It is a jewel best panned in Jon Levenson's studies on power and resurrection in Judaism. In *Death and Resurrection of the Beloved Son* and *Resurrection and the Restoration of Israel*, the Harvard professor shows that the jewel is bestowed on the world as Israel becomes *Ebed Yahweh*—the servant of God.[34]

As we scan Israel's story which is also ours, we can see how exodus from captivity enters the crystal complex—but resurrection of the dead? As Rosh Hoshanah and Ramadan, Yom Kippur and *Eid al-Adha*—coinciding this year—remind us, the Abrahamic, Mosaic, Christic, and Islamic journey is a winding road not yet made straight in the desert. Are the blind really given sight and the dead raised? Let's get real and painfully honest. In the history of God—particularly Jewish history—one of every two persons born since Jesus' time have—like him—been killed and have not lived out full lives. Are our Jewish forefathers raised from the incinerated dust of Auschwitz and the Rhineland synagogues? Do we all lie in the dust until final resurrection? In Hebrew faith, we find that kingdom of God—*Malchut Shamayim, Basileau tou theou*—is fragmentary, a filament, a dimly flickering wick—yet one that will not be put out—a light that cannot be quenched. We only see intimations of this grace of life. "In the midst of death we are in life."

Paul the Jew sees this mystery: "we who live are always being put to death for Jesus' sake—that the life of Jesus might be manifest in our mortal flesh" (2 Cor 4.11). "Our days are consumed in your wrath" proclaims our psalm. "We are as a tale that is told" (Ps 90.9).

In our time—*chronos*, God evidently does not fix our morbidities and mortalities: illness, loss, grief, failure. In addition to natural evils—acts of innocence, ignorance, and injustice—bad mortgages, foreclosures, insensitivities, and stupidities, deeds done and left undone—all stalk our way through life. As the great servant song of Isaiah 40 shows—the straight and smooth highway in the desert—the perfect Torah path—is a messianic bestowal. Under strictly human construction, it remains crooked and rocky.

Yet an oasis is set in the desert. Yes all flesh is grass but our iniquity is pardoned, our warfare accomplished and the glory of the Lord shall be revealed and all mortal flesh shall see the glory. Even wretched Job knew that in his mortal flesh he would see God. He knew that the righteousness of God was salvation and translation.

Finally, the wisdom we seek is a Gospel matrix—a Christian phenomenon. We find it in Jesus inaugural commentary at Capernaum

---

34. See Levenson, *The Death and Resurrection of the Beloved Son* and *Resurrection and the Restoration of Israel*.

on Isaiah 61—"I come to give sight to the blind, to set the prisoner free." Fulfilling messianic promise and Logos—Word made mortal flesh is signaled in Jesus' profuse healings and miracles. It's there you remember in the dispatch to John the Baptist on death row at Herod's palace: Are you the one to come or shall we look for another? "What do you see? The blind see, lepers are cleansed, the dead are raised and the poor receive good news." It colors his picture of last judgment: "when did we see you hungry and feed you, thirsty and give you the cup of water, naked and clothe you ... inasmuch as you did it to the least of these ... "

Jesus came that we who were lost and dead, full of fear and dread, might have life and life abundant. *Zoe aionion* ("life ages") has become *L'Chaim*. This early winter liturgical season concerns the coming out of God to be near us ... our neighbor ... Emmanuel, God with us. Messiah came out to this world ... born in the obscure Jewish outpost of the mighty Roman empire ... he taught, performed, and embodied the messianic gift. He searched the world in messianic desire—*domini canis*—the hound of heaven. He absorbed our human pretension and mistake ... our dreadful turn-away. He cried out: "Father forgive them they know not what they do." He healed and forgave, suffered and died, descended and ascended—then to return for good and ingratiate his beloved creature through his companion Spirit. Ultimately, he brings it back victorious and delivers the kingdom to his father. Thus the Father consummates the desire of the beloved son, satisfaction is won and by his knowledge the righteous servant justifies many.

Torah and *Taurut*, Gospel and *Injil*, Passover and *Parousia*—all Abrahamic *seminea* is realistic and fecund. It is heaven come down to earth to bring forth its fruit. The wisdom is sublimely knowable and eminently doable. The Gospel of God is near, so near—oil charism on our foreheads—in our dreams, sufferings and healings—in our ecstasies and abandonments. It invades our heads and thinking, our hearts and feeling, our mouths and speaking, our deaths and our departing. It companions—the bread and wine of life—manna in the wilderness. So with our Jewish kinsfolk at Yom Kippur we sing *Alenu* ... ("it is our duty") that we live to give praise for another year ... we give thanks ... Amen.

Meeks continues his analysis of the essence of the divine/human economy:

- Exodus/Easter, beyond its saving and redeeming power, is the definitive event in the economic history of God. It is repurchase, redemption, release from slavery. Saved from famine by Egyptian economic Vizier,

Joseph—their brother they sought to kill—God's chosen are brought back through the "death and resurrection of the beloved son," through the depression of scarcity in the wilderness to the Land flowing with milk and honey. This is not just a spiritual parable. It is God's intention for life from death, plenitude from scarcity—within and through the creation—for the enrichment of all of life.

- As Torah keepers, God's people seal and perpetuate their deliverance from the "house of bondage" to the service of justice-tenored abundance throughout the Household as the whole earth is filled with the Glory of God (Isa 11.9). Hospitality here is to the family and neighborhood, but also to the stranger and enemy. Torah becomes the charter of God and neighbor love. Stealing and killing, coveting and deceiving are no longer allowed to spoil the creation. Those whom we seek to abandon and starve to death through thoughtless policies (*e.g.*, Katrina and Gaza) will be delivered, fed, healed, and made to walk again, and there will be joy in heaven.

- The covenant of life (Torah is a political economy) with all humanity (Gen 9) sees murder, violence, injustice, and immorality as derivative of idolatry and blasphemy. Torah is a stern warning: "You shall not wrong a stranger or oppress him . . . You shall not afflict any orphan or widow . . . If you do, they will cry out to me and I will hear them, and my wrath will burn and I will kill you with the sword" (Exod 22.21–24). And you will not gouge or exploit the poor, nor charge him interest on debt. "If your brother becomes poor . . . you shall maintain him . . . Take no interest from him. You shall not lend him money at interest nor give him food for profit . . . I am the Lord your God. I brought you up from slavery" (Lev 25.35–38).[35]

The theology of economics formulated by professors Long, Tanner, and Meeks offers hints for a creative theology for today, one that will correct the deficient version I have exposed, one that will lead us out of danger into a day more like the "Day of the Lord," when judgment leads us to repentance and new resolve—to justice, love, and peace.

---

35. Meeks, *God the Economist*, 100–108.

ECOLOGY

A Theology of the Land

GOD'S RESOURCES

"Land is a central, if not *the* central, theme of biblical faith."[36] This profound claim is born out in the global crisis I seek to describe, analyze, and advise in this book and in the immediate context of this writing. Today, Israel lays waste to the *Terra Sancta* in biblical Gaza in blockade, bombing, and invasion. That glorious biblical coastland has now become an oppressive cage of enslavement for the Palestinian people—much like ancient Israel in Egypt. At the same time, the beleaguered Palestinians fire their makeshift rockets at Israel's sacred lands and homes, and both peoples of *Haaretz* tremble in fear.

In the other American crisis I have raised, homes and lands and their inhabitants also cry out. Paul Reyes writes in a recent issue of *Harper's Magazine*: "Between 2005 (the beginning of the foreclosure crisis in Florida) and 2008, the rates of homes being lost (foreclosed) had quadrupled to 35,000 per month."[37] We may assume that this *Landnahme* (seizure) has accelerated in the intervening months. I call this appropriation morally suspect because it has been unevenly visited on lower and middle classes, although in San Diego $10 million homes are being foreclosed. Reyes continues: "the collapse was surreal in its proportion, biblical in its egalitarian reach."

Evidently, the crisis in all its parameters is biblical in its reach to all peoples—great and small. It is a crisis of greed, arrogance, and violence. It all involves theft from the poor, usurpation, and dispossession of the people of the land. It also portends judgment and hope. It is the history of Israel, of Jesus, and Mohammed—all reenacted. The core question is that of the Niebuhrs and Barth—those spearheading a new biblical theology: What is God doing in His and therefore our world? And another neo-biblical theologian, Walter Brueggemann, gets it right when he names land the central theme of the Bible.

---

36. Brueggemann, *The Land*, 3.

37. Paul Reyes, "Bleak Houses: Digging Through the Ruins of the Mortgage Crisis," *Harper's Magazine*, October 2008.

Brueggemann is the world's preeminent Old Testament scholar after Gerhard von Rad. He comes from a similar ethos as the Niebuhrs one generation later: America's heartland—St. Louis, rural Missouri and Elmhurst college in Chicago's Western inner-suburbs. This is bungalow country. These tidy, tiny, one-floor brick homes were bought decades ago for $5,000 to $10,000 and appreciated to $300,000—bought by Hispanic and Asian families 20 years ago. Now their values have collapsed and the lawn workers, nannies, and McDonalds burger-flippers—the labor force that upholds our whole society—are feeling the pinch with mortgages often greater than the home's value. The American dream has turned into a nightmare.

In one of his 100 books, *Hope Within History*, Brueggemann lines out his system of biblical principles about land, economy, security, and home:[38]

- The goods and resources of the earth belong to God and through God become the heritage of all people and the creation.

- God abhors empires for their idolatry and injustice usurping divine Lordship over all of life.

- God's righteousness (*Tsadeqah*) is his "Goodness/Godness"—the very manifestation of His being in the world.

- God seeks human righteousness that is justice, love, truth, and peace (Rabbi Akiva). This righteousness is expressed through human social, political, and economic endeavors.

- Humans choose rather to grasp, cling, hoard, and protect what they have for themselves. This tends to prompt aggression and exploitation against other people and defensive security measures designed to protect possessions from, rather than share with, others.

> He looked for justice (*mishpat*)
> He found only bloodshed (*mispah*)
> He looked for righteousness (*Tsadeqah*)
> He found only a cry (*saqah*) (Isa 5.7)

According to Brueggemann, the economy, including land and nation, is given by God to people to serve the neighborhood. Humans are in covenant with God and neighbors—near and far—and this covenant occurs within an environment and economy. Torah and Decalogue, Gospel and

---

38. Brueggemann, *Hope Within History*.

Ethic, *Taurut* and *Ingil* (Arabic for "way" and "gospel") supply mandates for this covenant stewardship. We recall Yusuf Islam's manna-in-the-morning meditation. Fresh provision is laid out on the earth with the dew, provided new every day for the sustenance of all. If it is hoarded, blockaded (as in Gaza or other unethical, siege/war crimes), it rots away, is despoiled, and fails in its intended deliverance (Exod 16.14, John 6.31, 2 Cor 8.15).

In light of this biblical theology of land according to Brueggemann, we must ask why we try to create military-industrial states in the world to cordon off wealth to ourselves and then fashion security states to defend what we erroneously think is ours. In this heresy, we succumb to idolatry and injustice and ruin God's world by thwarting His intended providence.

The land theology of scripture should rather prompt us to private philanthropy, programs of industry, business, commerce, and economics that disperse, share, and provide for all and programs of law and policy that disallow the grotesque disparity arising between rich and poor, and wealthy and suffering nations in God's would-be provident world.

As political realists, Brueggemann and the Niebuhrs know we must seek to preserve justice, order, and peace in the world, averting conflict and war that rob people of their land, food, sustenance, and life itself. We must counter the aggression of gangs, corporations, tribes, nations, and empires in the name of the vulnerable, week, and needy for whom God contends through our witness. And in all our providing and protecting action, we must be ready to see the log in our own eyes as well as the speck in the eye of our neighbor. We must not turn our own nation into an idol.

Scriptural Reasoning and the Land

To flesh out the theology of land I am building from biblical grounds through the hermeneutics of Brueggemann, we first look at the ground-work proposal I make in this study to consult interfaith scriptural reasoning. In all religion, land is seen as the physical basis of fertility and life itself. God is the author of life and breath and He mediates these vitalities through the instrument of the good earth, sea, and sky with its creatures.

Land is a sacred trust in the three Abrahamic faiths. Land gives God a living body—a creation.[39] Land makes humanity the epitome of the creation in two senses: 1) humans become stewards of creation—caring and guiding creation toward fruition; and 2) humans become creation's ser-

---

39. See McFague, *The Body of God.*

vant, as one who reveres creation in God—its maker and sustainer—for the sustenance, life, health, and delight it provides. Creation depends on humans and humans on creation in a glorious and ominous reciprocity. For this reason, creation is shrouded in warning and command. This connection of creation and command in Torah is fundamental to each faith of Abraham. Consider the scriptural reasoning chain as it relates to land.

Hebrew Scripture

The Lord spoke to Moses and said, "Say unto your people . . . 'When you reap the harvest of your land, do not reap to the very edge of your field or gather the gleanings of your harvest . . . Do not go over your vineyard a second time . . . leave them for the poor.' I am the Lord your God . . . Do not steal. Do not lie. Do not deceive one another. Do not swear falsely by my name. Do not defraud your neighbor or rob him. I am the Lord" (Lev 19.9–14). "If you obey these commands and statutes . . . I will gather you back to the land I have given you." (Deut 30). "The earth is the Lord's and everything in it" (Psa 24).

Christian Scripture

"All power is given to me . . . on earth . . . Go to all nations and tell them to observe all that I have commanded you" (Matt 28).

Islamic Scripture

"There is no God but Allah who made the earth (for all) to live in." (Qur'an, Surah 27.61).

This *midrashic* chain (successive development and cross-referential elaboration) shows the clear affinity of the three sacred literatures, especially in light of the fact that Hebrew scripture, in at least one sense, is both Christian and Muslim scripture (cf. "Peoples of the Book"). The command structure is central to the significance of the land. Torah and its distillation into the pure *Verbum Dei*—the Decalogue—informs all the texts. The sage Nachmonides claimed the connection of the land of Israel, even its dirt and stones, with *mitzvoh*. The enduring message of biblical witness is that a theology of the earth is inextricably bound up with the commands of God that distill into the imperatives of undivided love of God and disinterested justice and love toward neighbor. A theology of the earth, therefore, is about commitment to the poor and refusing to steal, lie, deceive, defraud, and witness falsely against the neighbor. Why this rigorous *mitzvot*? "I am the Lord, your God."

For Christianity, the world and the land is the staging platform for the dissemination of the Gospel. This view leads some commentators to find a certain disdain for the earth and the land at least in contrast with the two Semitic sibling faiths. While there may be a more earthly worldly spirit in Judaism and Islam, Christianity is intensely committed to world, earth, and land by virtue of its doctrines of creation and incarnation. Christianity will be less invested in particular national homelands than Israel and Islam since it follows the "pilgrim-on-earth" doctrine of Apocalyptic Judaism, the other-worldliness of Plotinus and the neoplatonists, and the new creation of Paul and Augustine. With John's Apocalypse, we await a new heaven and new earth. Here we have no abiding city, and we remain strangers and sojourners on the earth. Yet this means only that we believe by faith we are citizens of heaven, part of the ecumenical fellowship that stretches across all lands and nations, the land we belong to being the whole earth.

Islam has some unique beliefs about land. Islamic vision is in part provincial—*Dar al-Islam* is the particular land(s) where the faith has enjoyed secular and political prominence and *Shariah* law is in place. It also believes that there are lands yet to be converted (*Dar al-Harb*), where faith is contested and war at least in the sense of greater *Jihad* (of mind and spirit) obtains.

Of course Arabia—Mecca and Medina—and the realms where Arabic and Qur'an run deep, are *Terra Sancta* in a special sense. The residence of the *Kaaba* is like the Jerusalem from which Mohammed ascended on the night journey—*Axis mundi*—the naval or center of the earth. Here the faithful circumambulate to complete the *Hajj*. Here was the primal place designated as the house for God by Abraham. This locus of the divine presence is where the angels descend and ascend on the ladder to heaven. Jerusalem also is sacred. Here is the place of the *Akedah* of Isaac and Ishmael. Surah 7 of the Qur'an acknowledges that Israel is given the promised land, although the deeper conviction is that this is the bequest to Abraham for the whole world of faith—Islam. The agonies of Palestine and Israel this Epiphany night—with deadly rockets and munitions streaking across the skies near Jerusalem—strangely recall the original meanings of angels and terror.

Neither Christianity nor Islam has theologies of restoring Israel in Palestine, yet from the earliest days of each movement—Helena and Constantine's churches; Holy Sepulchre and Nativity; and Islam's tropism toward and with Muslim Palestine—betray their deeper convictions. All three Abrahamic movements, it seems, believe, if only eschatologically, Buber's persuasion that this land (Zion) can only be holy if it is home to all faiths. Will the world be led up to the old Jebusite, then Davidic stronghold by the composite children of Abraham—and will we there beat "swords into plowshares" (Isa 2.4) or "plowshares into swords" (Joel 3.10)?

In *The Land*, Brueggemann pulls together a theology of land that guides my creative proposals in Part Four. His central themes are: a new biblical hermeneutic; biblical faith as storied faith (placed history); God of history, land, and covenant; generations and land in Christian and interfaith theology; homelessness and home: a Christian theology of home, land, the dispossessed and justice; and the landed and urban technocracy.

A new hermeneutic of land is required to get to a relevant and viable theology. The discipline of hermeneutics is the philosophical/theological activity of translating ideas and norms to form meanings and values into actual living issues in the world. The root hermeneutical issues about land concern issues of physics, *i.e.*, space and time as categories of thought about reality. Is the Bible about nature or history? Scholarship once emphasized nature—the Bible was about mountains, waters, fertility, moons, and stars. This came to be dismissed as nature-worship, pantheism—confusing Spirit with physical reality. Biblical hermeneutics then turned to history and story (narrative) as the medium comprehending the reality of God in the world. "The great acts of God" became the watchword for this approach. Exodus, land-settlement, exile, incarnation, resurrection—these great belief-occurrences became the foci of biblical interpretation. One hermeneutic negated land as dirt and location, the other—land as memory and hope.

Brueggemann was among the pioneer biblical scholars to avoid both univocal approaches. He proposed focusing on scripture as worldly theology—"storied faith" or "placed history." In his unique blend of concrete Judaism (historical and natural) and Mircea Eliade's typology of universal myth (cosmic and eternal/recurring), J.Z. Smith argues that place (land) has meaning because history is lodged there. We can no longer accept the antithesis of God of history and gods of the land. "As Yahweh is Lord of events, so he is also fructifier of the land. As he comes in 'that Day,' so also he watched over the land."[40] On this day of worldwide celebrations of the "Three Kings" and the elusive phenomenon of Epiphany, Jews and Muslims explode rockets over the land where Bethlehem's "Nativity" stars once shone—evidencing the enduring importance of Brueggemann's hermeneutical breakthrough.

Scripture always seeks to reside truth and God in a specific place and in universal transcendence—thus pertaining to one and all—to the least and greatest. Sinai, Israel, Jerusalem, Bethlehem, Nazareth, and again Jerusalem—all little nowheres on the stage of secular history: Babylon, Athens, Rome, Paris, London, Berlin, Washington, Moscow, Beijing, New York, Mumbai. Yet, to paraphrase a well-known piece—all the armies that ever marched, the ships launched, the cables dispatched, the monies possessed—together have had only slight influence compared to that pioneer trekker, the "one solitary life" of Abraham. May it be, Brueggemann asks, whether only the provincial can be universal and must not the eternal also be local?

Today a political circus plays out in one of those worldly *megalopolai*, where princes of the earth strut their silly pretensions. Chicago's Roland Burris, former State Attorney General, has accepted the nomination from discredited Governor Rod Blagojevich, to fill Barack Obama's vacated Senate seat. As with President Bush's "divine call" to invade Iraq, Burris claims divine chosenness. Apropos my point on sacred place, I am forced to quip: When 'either/or' logic obtains, the question becomes whether Roland was ordained to Barack's seat by God or by Rod. Brueggemann asks of us more subtlety, for surely "My thoughts are not your thoughts nor are My ways your ways" (Isa 55.8).

Brueggemann is a Christian theologian. Scripture for him is the Bible Jesus knew, *i.e.* Hebrew *Tanakh*—some Hebrew and perhaps Aramaic texts—perhaps the Septuagint (LXX) and the *Tanakh* (*Torah, Nabim, Ketubim*) in Greek. To this is added the New Testament—Gospels, Paul, Letters, and Apocalypse. His theology of land thus reflects this inter-scriptural perspective. The distinctive Christian elements we find here are built on the core distinctive Judaic themes of history, covenant, generationality, and land.

"Generations" and "land-as-inheritance" are Judaic themes somewhat in tension with Christian themes, although they ultimately flow to-

---

40. Brueggemann, *The Land*, 185.

gether from the same scriptural spring. Jews are genetic, ethnic, biological descendents of Jacob or Abraham. This belief is born out in generational lines. Such genealogical continuity is connected with the land and with the Diaspora. Our fathers came out of Egypt, celebrated Passover, sojourned in the desert, encamped at Sinai, and together made the Exodus, and this is more than a spiritual affinity—in a very real sense, we were there. Something of the same organic connectivity also is found in the Semitic Arabs of Islam, although that faith community has become as impressively diverse—with an ethnicity and theology as expansive as Christianity. Christians have been deeply shaped by the Judaic theology of land, and Jews have incorporated many Christian insights.

Those Christian theological understandings focus on the dispossessed and broad issues of universal justice. Christian reflections on the land have been shaped by the prophetic Jewish tradition through the dialogue with Marxism in socialist Europe, Orthodox Russia, Confucionist China, and revolutionary South America. Marx and Engels were theological/philosophical thinkers whose work, though heavily atheistic in tone, was deeply influenced by the Hebrew prophetic and biblical heritage and the German Christian and pastoral (Shephardic and land-based) tradition.

Christians can only engage in the agonizing issues of Israeli wars with Palestine and Gaza—as well as the tensions and travail Israel experiences with Islamic Iran and Islamic/Christian Syria, Iraq and Lebanon—to the extent that we fathom the depths of Israel's association with the homeland, as her Diaspora existence throughout the world has largely been and remains repudiated by the Christian and Muslim worlds. The three faiths converge in their belief and hope in the land of promise and in their conviction that the land is a gift not to be presumed upon as a possession, but received with stewardship on behalf of the whole world. The land is gift not only to the children of Abraham, but to the world of faith as an "arena of justice and freedom."[41]

The theme of "homelessness" captures this interfaith awareness, especially the Christian sensibility based as it is on the experience of the Messiah (anointed One) who had "nowhere to lay his head." The currency of this idea resonates with the theme of justice. Holy land is about God's love for the weak, vulnerable, oppressed, children, the sick, homeless, voiceless, and poor (Exod 2.23–25). Those whose existence is denied and/

41. Brueggemann, *The Land*, 191.

or negated are the particular focus of God's homemaking provision—the wretched victims of war and violence in Gaza and in the broader theatre of Israel/ Palestine epitomize this understanding of holy land as *sub specie aeternitatis (Deus)* ("under the aspect of eternity").

God is in alliance with the poor against the landed. The God who has given the land has given it for the protection and sustenance of those whose cry he has heard and will not deny. Jesus' crucifixion is the experience of being dispossessed and rendered homeless. In vindication of God's beloved Son, God has made the land a refuge for his anointed and afflicted peoples. What this means and entails for his chosen children of Abraham and the Messianic entourage God is forming in the world at large and in *Haaretz Israel*—in Emmanuel Logos—for Jews, Christians and Muslims—is now unfolding in time and space. It will always remain an eschatological mystery—a land of promise as God's world awaits kingdom come, the new land, new creation come down from heaven.

Land for now—including Israel/ Palestine—also is a spirit-event, a development of biblical import and magnitude that bears on the history of America in God's world. The following meditation, arising from my work at the Center for Advanced Religious and Theological Studies at Cambridge, reflects on the meaning of what is unfolding before us.

Two Camps

It is indeed a tale of two cities—full of damnation and redemption—fully Dickensian. A several-month sojourn in Europe recently had made me aware of a coalescence of global forces that portend such a double-edged sword during the fateful election year of 2008. An uncanny and most uncomfortable instinct told me that the world was gathering into two clashing communities—The U.S. and Israel on the one hand, Europe and Islam on the other—in what is now being called "Eurabia."[42]

A possible intermediacy third party—among Russia, India and Pakistan, China, Africa, and the Muslim world—is standing in the wings of the UN, the global economy, the international court, the laws of the seas, and every other glimmer of the truth that we shall one day be a global community—God's people in this one world that belongs to His redemptive way and sway.

---

42. See Jenkins, *God's Continent.*

This coming world may seem quite out of sorts with the all-too-evident *realpolitik,* as Iran tests her rocket delivery systems, and Israel and the U.S. discuss preemptive strike. In this bleak midwinter, Pakistan/India becomes a cauldron where the once munificent medieval *madrassas* ("schools") now become smoking factories for insurgents and terrorists, Western "torture schools" (with their Catholic links) contort the bitter legacy of old Franco-Algerian colonial systems into something now commensurable with Islamic "suicide schools," and one of the greatest humanistic writers of our generation, Nobel laureate Harold Pinter, calls Blair and Bush to dock for war crimes. All around us, the noble Abrahamic residue of Avicenna, Maimonides, and Aquinas—the whole world God made and said, "It is good," the beloved world Christ came to redeem—whirls as Loren Eiseley envisioned into a Dante-like Inferno.

The gathering storm I see is far different from that envisioned by a "clash of civilizations" between the West and Islam or America and the Hispanic world in Huntington's last Manichaean apocalypse. This crisis is focused in the very heartland of Euro-American culture. Let us glance into this crisis through the eyes of two important new studies in biblical theology—referring also to two religious developments that seek to engage dialogue on the Christian/Muslim issue. My purpose is to endorse the interfaith dialogue, all the while calling for a firmer commitment to begin trialogue with attention to biblical and historical Israel. As I will show later, Israel's absence from pan-Abrahamic sharing now takes the theological heart away from public discourse and threatens to render it vacuous and irrelevant.

I have become aware in these precarious years of something Israel has known for 4,000 years—how fragile her existence is in the world. One of every two Jews born since the earthly life of Jesus the Jew has been killed and not allowed to live out his or her God-given life. Today, the American misadventure in the invasion and occupation of Iraq and the further, equally misinformed venture contemplated in Iran, has accelerated again the centripetal cleansing and refugee process. To this is added the Israeli attack, occupation, and dismemberment of Palestine and the furtive and futile attack on Lebanon (2006) and Gaza (2008–2009) that makes it feel that America is the only friend Israel has left in the world. Nine percent of all Jews left in the world are now in America and Israel. This is something like the concentration of global Jewry exiled in Eastern Europe 150 years ago. I am told that there are only some 30 Jews left in

Cairo, a once-thriving synagogue city, and that pattern holds throughout the Islamic world.

Equally disturbing to the *Shoah* and the dejudification of *Dar al-Islam* is the de-Christianization of Israel and Palestine. A once-20-percent population is now less than 1 percent. Long gone is the pattern of centuries past when the "Peoples of the Book" harbored each other in freedom and safety as in medieval *Al-Andalus*. Though the Jewish community is impressive in France, England, and Holland (400,000, 200,000, and 100,000, respectively), these communities are feeling increasingly embattled and uncomfortable, especially as Islam surges into the spiritual vacuum that is modern secularized and materialistic Europe.

The immediate background to this crisis is obviously the tripartite, fratricidal intra-Abrahamic conflict caused by the mania in Israel for a security state, tenored by a terrible Holocaust revenge. This is seconded by the same craving for an idolatrous security state in the U.S., tinged by an insufferable and ill-targeted revenge and belligerence animated by September 11th. This theo-global mania, we must remember, is fueled as much by dispensational Christian theology and militant Islam as by the "Israel Lobby."

And finally, swept into the cauldron are the blasphemous, yet *Mullah*-unchallenged and unhindered suicide bombings of innocent civilians by militant Muslims in every corner of the world. What is anathema and unethical in each Abrahamic faith and its "Just War" tradition, has now been glorified as heroic martyrdom.

So where can we look for hope, justice, peace, and salvation? My thesis throughout this writing is that the confession of the Jewish people and the name of the God of Israel must endure in the world for the world itself, so that the soul of humanity can continue and fulfill its redemptive destiny. Judaism conveys into history the theological and ethical substance of both Christianity and Islam. A bilateral Christian-Muslim dialogue is not only insufficient—it sends an ominous signal to the world. To insure a broader triune context, the Abrahamic family of faiths must reverse its recent historical course of enmity as we now offer amity and go to the wall for Israel, opposing the wall, as Dietrich Bonhoeffer did in that "greater love . . . for his friends." (John 15.13). Conceptually and ethically, we must reanchor our convictions, not in hatred and supercessionism, but in the truth of God and in the derivative humanistic ethical substance that we all share.

THE COMMON BIBLICAL MATRIX

The resolution of this conflict can only come by the combined power of revelatory and rational ethics. We must take the deep pacific meanings of biblical apocalyptic (*e.g.*, Mark 13, Daniel, and Revelation), and join them to the canons of Just War theory to find this synergy. I derive this synthesis from two of the salient biblical and historical works now circulating: Robert Jewett's *Hermeneia* Commentary on Romans and Martin Goodman's landmark *Rome and Jerusalem*.[43] Each, in his own way, is dealing with a contemporary interpretation of what Goodman presciently calls "an ancient clash of civilizations." Along with Rodney Stark's *Cities of God*,[44] these works encourage the search for a modern relevance of their work.

JUDAISM AND CHRISTIANITY: SYNERGISTIC DESTINY

Robert Jewett had to be barred by his colleagues from taking another five years to add an Italian bibliography to work that was already 25 years in the making and bring his "Romans" to a close. The conclave was in our living room in Evanston. At the end of that night, we acknowledged that the quarter century was well spent, as the book could now join the historically crucial commentaries of the same epistle by Luther and Barth—to say nothing of Augustine and Wesley—all of which helped guide the world through ominous times.

Acutely aware of Greco-Roman rhetorical theory and finding evidence of a modern sociological template of honor and shame, Jewett has cleared up long-standing biases by those who appropriated the passages from the Greek Septuagint and deliberately changed the meanings of the Hebrew text. With his protégée James Dunn, he also has forged a fully affirmative treatment of the people Israel in the world, free from the now-embarrassing anti-Judaic tone of previous German scholarship.

Two features of his study bear on my thesis. He first takes a view toward religious zeal expressed in terms of violence and then offers a positive perspective of Israel's political destiny in world history and the country's enduring provenance in the care and purposes of God. He also addresses America's pretensions to power in the world.

Knowing this good colleague for many years has convinced me of the theology about violence that undergirds all of his work. He is a disciple of the peaceful Christ. Convicted by the non-retaliative forgiveness

43. See Jewett, et al., *Romans: A Commentary* and Goodman, *Rome and Jerusalem*.
44. See Stark, *Cities of God*.

of *Ecce Homo*, the cross of Christ in its Pauline construal becomes the *sine qua non* of all Jewett's exegesis. I often have heard him reflect on Judas and the zealots and how they wrongly and abruptly sought to rupture the kingdom into premature being. In his many studies preliminary to *Captain America and the Crusade Against Evil* (with John Lawrence),[45] he has forwarded a position of Pauline conciliation with the powers of Rome—resistance to Rome's blasphemy and Judacide, yes, but otherwise living in equanimity with the powers that be as the Jewish people did under Babylon and Persia where the great Talmudic period would flourish.

It is true that Jesus seemed to believe that state violence was inevitable in the concourse of the Gospel and that he and his disciples would be killed no matter how pacifist their response was to Rome. This was part of the larger concession to divine plan wherein with Peter's confession he turns his face "steadfastly toward Jerusalem" (Mark 10.33). But Jewett takes numerous passages: "put up your sword" (Matt 26), the prediction of the fall of the walls of Jerusalem (Mark 13), and the cleansing of the temple (Luke 19.45) to indicate that Jesus sought to avert the calamity that Goodman depicts in his lachrymose history where Jewish (and Christian) blood flowed like rivers down from Mt. Zion (Josephus).[46]

Beyond the first level of argument that is pacifist and consequentionalist, Jewett moves to a deeper theological argument that embraces the ethical. Rejecting the radical apocalyptical line of Pauline/Augustinian clash of two cities for a more irenic cohabitation, Jewett develops his argument in two further steps to show that Israel and the church have a synergistic destiny to complement each others' unique place in the plan of God.

He first shows that the offering for the poor of Judea (Rom 15.25–26) reveals the inextricable reciprocity of thanksgiving toward one's ancestral people and the further success of the Gospel. If the mission to Spain is to go forward, if one day those gladiatorial lands are to know of the righteousness of God, the mission of help to the poor of Jerusalem—a Gentile offering—must go back to Judea and Paul will deliver it in person. The Jerusalem community, we can believe, included James, Jesus' brother, with whom Paul had undergone such strife (Acts 15), the Jewish Christians (if such a designation is possible), Jesus' extended family, and the associated Jewish community with whom archeology shows Christians may have shared a

45. See Jewett and Lawrence, *Captain America.*
46. See Goodman, *Rome and Jerusalem.*

common *mikvah/* baptismal bath and perhaps even worship quarters at the Western gate of the city. Jewett finds Paul's explication of a divine theology of Jerusalem and Rome one of reciprocity rather than mutual recrimination. The apostle develops this theology in Romans (ch. 10–11).[47]

Building on the foundational argument of Jesus Messiah as the purveyor of righteousness and peace and the pastoral/ethical imperative of mutual, physical aid, within and beyond the particular faith community, Jewett next traces Paul's contentions about Judeans (Jews) and Romans (Gentiles) to a subtle camaraderie they share in the sacrifice offering of Messiah and the radical brotherhood this engenders in the *hikmah* ("wisdom") of God. The position unfolds in three parts: 1) the equality of Jew and Gentile under divine justice and grace; 2) the "call" therefore to Jew and Greek to present worship as "bodies of living sacrifice" (12.1); since 3) this "political formation" is the pattern of divine life for this world.

Equality of Jews and Gentiles

The stated purpose of Paul's Letter to the Romans, writes Jewett, is to set forth "the equality of Jew and Gentile under sin and grace and stress the inclusive rule of faith." While this may sound like all the other "Lutheran" works on Romans, it marks a radical departure. Jewett is arguing for a radical parity among the offspring of Abraham in the absolute fairness, equity, and desire of God for the righteousness and salvation of His Jewish and Gentile children. This radical equity and parity is all the more remarkable given Paul's experience of being:

- attacked in Galatia by "the Judaizers";
- confronted by sharp exchange with Peter at Antioch (Gal 2.14);
- attacked by Jewish/Christian missionaries at Corinth (2 Cor 10–13); and
- physically tortured by fellow Jews (2 Cor 11.24).

Like Jesus, Paul was considered a criminal. The 39 lashes—administered five times—left gashes (*stigmata tou Jesou*) on his body (cf. Isa 53). He was accused of breaking synagogue custom, claiming Torah was no longer effectual. In Goodman's view, Jesus was accused of repudiating and invalidating Jewish religion, *per se*, which was precisely what the Roman

---

47. See *L'exégèse patristique de Romains 9–11.*

Empire attempted when they desecrated and destroyed Jerusalem and did not rebuild it—as had been their custom in other conquests.[48]

Rome's pogrom sought to eradicate Judaism itself, not just the Jewish people. But Paul forcefully objects: "far be it," "God forbid," "No way!" and "this is not what I'm about." His conviction and commission was the exact opposite. Throughout his correspondence, he seeks to "uphold the law." His ministry as such seeks to fulfill the Abrahamic vision of Israel (Torah, Moses, the Prophets, and Psalms). His proclamation is the "Gospel of God" (Rom 1.1)—the charter of righteousness and salvation, forgiveness of sin, and the renewal and rectification of life.[49]

Not only in apocalyptic writings but in legal and ethical literature, Judaism searches out the connection between righteousness, duty, death, resurrection, and the historical-worldly context of redemption—this world and the world to come. Rome's genocide of Jews, like that of twentieth-century Christendom in Europe, is a blasphemous assault on the "God of Israel"—on God's self.

In this light, both Jewett and Goodman are correct. The accusation against Paul was unjust. The Roman judgment was wrong—a "tragic accident."[50] The "parting of the ways" was an historical calamity, and the Jew and Gentile covenants of life under the God of Israel and in Jesus Messiah remain intact. Indeed, the wider family of Jew and Gentile that arose from the rift—Sara and Hagar, Isaac and Ishmael—remains a synergistic work of Torah and Task, Grace and Gospel, *Taurit* and *Injil*. In the enigmatic words of Dietrich Bonhoeffer, written days before his execution, fundamentally rejecting "the final solution," he wrote, "God rescued Israel from Egypt so that she might live with him on earth, forever."[51] Israel is woven into the very fabric of Christ's messianic redemption of the world.

Living Sacrifice

This persuasion leads to Paul's theology of body-sociologic, ecclesiologic, and politic. Jewett proceeds to explore the cosmic divine rationale behind this sublime concord, now so obfuscated by historical inter-religious strife so profound that it mimics the divine entry into time and space in creation

---

48. Goodman, *Rome and Jerusalem.*

49. See Levenson, *The Death and Resurrection*; *Sinai and Zion*; *Resurrection and the Restoration*; and "Resurrection in the Torah."

50. Goodman, *Rome and Jerusalem.*

51. Bonhoeffer, *Letters and Papers from Prison.*

and incarnation. The proper offering (*logikon*) of Israel and extended Israel in this messianic age is an atmosphere of justice and rapport where our "bodies" are presented unto God as a "living sacrifice" (Rom 12.1).

Martin Buber affirmed in his study, *On Zion*, that the singular purpose of Israel in history is to witness to the light of justice and "love of the other."[52] Christians share that eternal bond with Jews—a marturial (living sacrifice) witness against the genocidal and Judacidal pretensions, idolatries, and violence of Rome and all her imperial successors. The bodily offering of Jewish and Christian resistance in the three-century span—Maccabees-*Bar Kochba* (150 BCE to 150 CE)—now is transfigured into a spiritual worship, a theocentric way of life. Sacrifice has been made ethical as the parochial cult realizes its universal destiny and opportunity. Christian Rome is built within the bosom of Diaspora Judaism. Rome is God's judgment and forgiveness on paganism, within which a Godless world is restored to the "Bosom of Abraham." Now—as in the story of Dives and Lazarus—righteousness and the "world beyond" is restored to the continuum of "here-and-now" sufferings and pains of this world.

Legacy of Abrahamic Theology

Today, if we indulge in a bit of conjecture, we find three imperial or quasi-imperial entities contending for political and economic preeminence and influence in the world. There is the Americo-Israeli world—very tenaciously holding its sway in the Middle East and in the global economy. Europe or Eurabia is emerging as a strong, but still precarious entity, given the enormous diversity of nations being swept formatively together out of an agonizing Eurasian history—including the ethically and theologically signature event of the Jewish *Shoah*. Then there are the rapidly developing and formidable neutral nations of Russia, China, India (scene of the most acute spiritual/cultural exacerbation), and the poorest of the poor and sickest of the sick—Africa.

I believe that monotheistic or Abrahamic faith holds the sway of the future. Of course Hinduism, Buddhism, and secularism, as well as the Chinese ways of life—all exert enormous global influence along with their precursors and successors. I see these as great universal, humanistic philosophies or ethics of life rather than theologies in the strict sense or monotheisms.

---

52. See Buber, *On Zion*.

In one way or another, the seed or offspring of Israel will determine the shape of world history given the enormous energy of evangelical and Pentecostal Christianity and of global Islam—especially in the epicenters of Indonesia and Asia, the Middle East, Africa, India/Pakistan, and Europe. I believe that the legacy of Abrahamic theology and justice is now becoming a singular phenomenon and has a chance to renew this inhabited and technologically unified world by muting violence, materialism, and exploitation and extending stewardship, justice, care, and hope—the phenomenon of redemption. Will we turn from enmity to amity—before it is too late? That is the question.

From the foundation of the earth—in the universal annunciation of the destiny of Abraham, in the selection and formation of the people of Israel by her God in Moses and the prophets, in the opportunity of the Greco-Roman *oikumene* and the broad universal cosmos it has formed and is yet forming in world history—the One God is seeking. Through the Hebrew, then universal messianic Being (*kaine ktisis* or "new creation") of humanity, God seeks to craft the *Tikkun Olam*, the kingdom of God, the way the world was meant to be and will in the certainty of redemption surely be. In this offering, the self-giving God and responsive humanity find "satisfaction of the soul" (Isa 53) as in the gift of *agapeto*—"He who did not spare his only beloved Son but freely gave him up, now in him freely gives the world all things" (Rom 8.23).

A JEWISH PERSPECTIVE

In his two cities, Martin Goodman explores the same theology of history from a Jewish perspective.[53] Following his work for many years as the professor of Jewish history in the train of his mentor Géza Vermes at Oxford, I have had the privilege of watching his perspective unfold as he oversaw the Cambridge History of Judaism, taught the Jewish Diaspora, and incorporated those dimensions into the new phenomenon of the State of Israel and the new Americo-European Jewish reality. Consider Goodman's reading of the ancient "clash of civilizations" exemplified in biblical Jerusalem and imperial Rome—and the legacies of empires and the perennial plight of the Abrahamic families of faith.

---

53. Goodman, *Rome and Jerusalem.*

Clash of Civilizations

Goodman reflects on the history of Emperor (to be) Vespasian sending his son Trajan to end the uprising in Judea and Palestine, with supposedly no intent to destroy the temple, only to have the attack end with its total destruction. A bloodbath of unprecedented fury by marauding soldiers ended with a declaration of the defeat of the Jewish religion, the taking of the paraphernalia of the temple (including the great Menorah candelabra and the Holy scrolls), parading them through the streets of Rome and displaying them on *l'Arc de Triomphe*. The *herem* ("accursed") signaled that the Jews and their faith were totally reviled. Genocide had accomplished deicide—or had it?

Rather than rebuilding the temple as was customary, the Emperor Hadrian built a pagan city, *Aelia Capitolina* in 132 CE, from which all Jews were banned. This total ostracizing of Jews, Goodman reasons, caused Christians to distance themselves from what was left of the Jewish community. Despite this point, it must be acknowledged that the New Testament never saw the destruction of the temple as a sign of God's judgment on Israel. At the same time, though, the Jewish Diaspora in Syria, Egypt, Asia Minor, and Rome did not join the zealot uprising. Perhaps Appian's record of 240,000 Jews being massacred in Cyprus would explain this reluctance. Before long, Jews and Christians would anathematize and excommunicate each other and the modern travail—crusade and ghetto, reformation and reviling, trifurcation and Holocaust—would be underway.

Perennial Plight of Abrahamic Faiths

It may be the case then, if this argument is valid, that a pagan empire projected its blasphemy, idolatry, and immorality—its composite violence toward God and humanity—toward the destruction of faith and the obliteration of the Divine Name from Israel. Here we see the importance of our marturial witness (*martys* in Greek, "martyr"), as each Abrahamic faith lays down its life for the validity and perpetuity of the Name of the One God of Israel, Jesus as Messiah, and Allah. Against this deicidal propensity and holocaust of empire, synagogue, church, and mosque must cry "never, never again!" Late Judaism and early Christianity are born in apocalyptic literature Richard Horsley sees as theological response to imperial oppression.

Note must be made here of very recent efforts at *rapprochement* among the three sibling faiths. In the contemporary language of war crimes against God and humanity—in truth commissions, repentance, reparations, and forgiveness—the churches have acknowledged sins and crimes against the Jews. Reconciliation documents have come from the Catholics, Lutherans, and Presbyterians, among others. Response documents including Vatican II (1960s), "*Dabru Emet*" (2000), and "A Common Word" (2006) from Jewish and Muslim leaders have furthered the reconciliation process.

One is forced to wonder, in light of my analysis of the very recent literature represented by Jewett and Goodman, whether this ecclesiastical remonstrance really carries much weight. Has anti-Semitism, anti-Islamism and anti-Christianity seeped into the secular waters of empire where they now pollute all culture despite the lachrymose confessions and pleadings of religious bodies and well-intentioned scholars? Has society had enough—30 years, 100 years—of wars of religion?

Two camps, two cities—where do they leave us? Two scenarios it would seem lie before us. Scenarios are dreams, constructions, imaginations, films. They are confabulations or construals within the human mind—personal and collective. The mind is always the receptor, interceptor, and conceptor of wide ranging impressions, ideas, divinities, and interpretations. Various subconscious or subliminal patterns and processes intercede and involve—depending on how one assesses psychological process, (*e.g.*, Freud)—with this array of impulses. My pre-dawn dreams are the most vibrant, creative and regrettably, also most distorted versions of reality within my imagination. Dawn brings depression, but also graceful release from morbid fantasy.

Most human thoughts, theories, literatures, songs, ideas, and other expressions flow from this wellspring. The Book of Revelation is a film—a running stream of consciousness and conscientiousness. The Book of Daniel, Mark 13, and all pieces of apocalyptic literature are dramas. Hearing Scottish actor Alan McCown recite Mark's Gospel in a West End theatre makes this clear. Apocalypses—apparently bad dreams—capture very sensible ethical wisdom such as that embodied in the Decalogue.[54] Utopias, dystopias, and plans are more comprehensive attractions or aversions. Scenarios are replays or foreplays of such irrepressibly human impulses. As persons and communities, we live in faith and hope that become the modalities by which we challenge the unknowns of daily real-

54. See *Die Dekalogische Struktur der Apokalypse* to explore how Bible passages reflect the Ten Commandments.

ity. We also confront omnipresent temptations that activate the vector of goodness or justice that is love.

We are also idealists as well as naturalists—Platonists and Aristotelians. Like Augustine, we know that the city of earth drops down from heaven as the city of heaven arises from the earth. We transfigure immanence by transcendence as well as transcendence by immanence.

The scenarios that follow from our reflections on Jerusalem and Rome—the two paradigmatic urban utopia/dystopias, of earthly or heavenly good or bad place—therefore follow Augustine's rather than Tertullian's more severe interpretation. Here, Jerusalem is the symbol of the city of peace, the city of God, and Rome symbolizes the earthly city, the city of conflict. These concluding theological images help us form a constructive theology of America's place in God's world.

City of Peace

The city of peace is the place where justice grounds concord because trust prevails over fear. For 60 years now, an interfaith reconciliation has been sought in the state of Israel, with Palestinian and Arab/ Muslim neighbors—guaranteed by the world community of nations. The present discord of faiths and peoples reflects a millennial/ perennial crisis and yearning. *Civitas Dei*—being about Church in the world—is an old woman who is becoming a young bride. It is the field of wheat and tares, sorting of sheep and goats, the old becoming new, the possible, actual—the proleptic, ontic—as Being itself transfigures being and "the kingdoms of this world become the kingdom of our God and of His messiah and He shall reign forever" (Rev 11).

In penultimate terms, which is the grammar of the Letter to the Romans, a justification and righteousness is being fashioned here and now upon the earth as people become just and righteous in the new being known as *Logos*, *Hikmah*, Sophia, Messiah. New being in God enables persons and peoples to live in care, respect, forgiveness, and forbearance rather than the much easier and more pleasurable (Augustine) rage, revenge, power, and violence—what Jewett characterizes as "shame" culture. The two-way process (Deut 8, Prov 14, Matt 5–7) is that described in Torah and Prophets, in Gospel—in *Taurut* and *Injil*—of annunciated goodness, of temptation, of grace-borne awareness of injustice and sin, of forgiveness, death and resurrection, of new being and new life—the completion of creation and kingdom. "New earth" is realization of what the world was meant to be. Now the earth brings forth its fruit, and justice and peace flourish.

The Worldly City

The worldly city—as Reinhold Niebuhr and the political realists rightly point out—is a place of treachery, deceit, and exploitation. Scriptural reasoning among faith adherents has a better chance of tipping the scales toward heavenly Jerusalem than do Versailles, Yalta, The Hague, and Annapolis. Yet try we must. American apocalyptic must be corrected by European (*e.g.*, Kant-Habermas) logic.[55] There may be rhyme, reason, even revelation, in the polar antinomy with which I began this essay. Eurabia and Americo-Israel may be providential configurations in the One in whose hands are the times and places of persons and peoples (Matt 16.3). Better to venture peace than crave animosity—to love and lose—than to choose not to love at all.

Two Provisional Moments

To conclude, I touch on two efforts in our earthly city to effect part of the called-for "coming together" under one "Common Word." Don Wagner, Director of the Center of Middle East Studies at North Park University, leads a group of "evangelical" Christian leaders in dialogue with Muslims through his partner—Mahmoud Ayoub, formerly of Temple University. A major conference in Libya brought together scholars from Britain and the U.S., as well as leaders from the Middle East. If this conference can help evangelicals sort out how its own belief structures and preaching are fueling inter-Abrahamic animosity and derivative discord in the world, the venture will have been well worth the effort. The belief that Messiah is resurrected and Logos reigns eternally may be fully orthodox, even to our Abrahamic sibling faiths. The elaborate Middle Eastern end-time eschatology is mischievous and theologically suspect. If evangelical faith can be cleansed of its nationalistic and cultural biases and find release in authentic biblical convictions, great strides toward world concord will have been made. This is one task before us as we seek to discern and direct America to a rightful place in God's World.

Our scriptural reasoning movement—radiating out of Cambridge, Virginia, and Princeton with cells and outposts around the world—has

---

55. See Habermas, *The Divided West.*

now assisted in the preparation of and presented responses to "A Common Word" from world Muslim leaders.[56] Thousands of official and informal house groups around the world now supply this endeavor. In my own experience, the simple sharing of viewpoints, both learned and "common sense" insights—which arise from a comparative read of cognate texts from Jews, Christians and Muslims—offers extraordinary enlightenment.

CONCLUSION

These two programmatic efforts are signature endeavors to make a difference and are examples of where we must begin. I have given hints of the theological and ethical menu we will put before our nation and world as we struggle to find our role in God's world. With the help of the best thinkers on the theology of nations, economics, and land, I have suggested the outlines of a helpful theology to respond to crises in which we are mired and which offer some promise of giving us new direction. We now turn to that final part of our study.

---

56. See Peter Ochs, "Speaking the Truth (*Dabru Emet*)," October 14, 2007 (Jewish Responses) and Kenneth L. Vaux, "Comment on the Document 'Common Word,'" October 2007 (Christian Responses) on the Web site of A Common Word, www.acommon word.com.

Constructive Theological and Ethical Directions

SECURITY

A New Politics

INTRODUCTION

CONTRADICTIONS ABOUND. THE PRESIDENTIAL inauguration is one week away. Obama's first order will be to close Guantanamo. There will be celebration around the world—satisfaction and shame at home. Outgoing President Bush ponders his legacy: Despite a 23-percent approval rating, he feels—along with millions of Americans—that "he done good." He would claim credit for the success of the surge in the Middle East, AIDS initiatives in Africa, and no new terrorist attacks at home. Others demand that he cry the Chicago playground *mea culpa*—"my bad!" because the economy is in shambles. Many poor and middle-class Americans have lost jobs and homes. Moderate income professionals like us have lost 30 to 40 percent of our assets—home value, retirement savings, and investments. Then there is Katrina. Esteem abroad wanes. And in the neglected Middle-East, blood flows and buildings fall in Gaza and, although the UN Secretary cries stop, the U.S. and Israel press on—with no hope that Obama will change course. And his inauguration is a week away. It is "the bleak midwinter, snow on snow."[1]

Hope and despair coexist. A "stimulus package" is promised. Three million new (replacement) jobs are promised. Towering deficits rise on top of towering deficits. Our children and grandchildren will pay the

---

1. Gustav Holst, "In the Bleak Midwinter," lyrics by Christina Georgina Rosetti, performed by E. Beckett, et al., *Holst: Orchestral Music*, Arte Nova Records, 1998 (compact disc).

price. Three new babies in our clan. Hallelujah! Snow on snow. Though some grumble, now most want to help. And in simple Bethlehem hope, we whisper: "What can I give him, poor as I am? If I were a shepherd I would bring a lamb. If I were a wise man, I would do my part. Yet what can I give him—give my heart."[2]

Now this so called "wise man"—feeling more like stumbling, bungling Kasper (the holy fool of the three kings)—is ready to take you into a final part of this theological journey. I wonder whether Obama, in addition to Guantanamo will also scrap Bush/Cheney's covert operations in Iran and Pakistan. What of preemptive cyber-warfare on China? Amid these quandaries, I have offered a diagnosis and prognosis of what I perceive to be the malady of America's being and mission in the world. I have sought prescriptive help from experts in three specialities to get us started toward recovery. Now, in the terms of a recent medical report, I propose to get the ICU patient up and walking—even though he remains in critical condition. Dangerous? Perhaps—but it is the way we must go, for we have miles to go before we sleep and "miles to go before I sleep."

A New Politics

Now 70 years old, having celebrated a birthday always buried in the exhaustion and weariness of the week after the new year, I have spent much of the last year campaigning for and unofficially advising Obama. I have traversed the nation with a booklet on "The Theology of the Presidential Candidates,"[3] which generated some good discussion of "citizenship" at colleges and churches in Indiana, Wisconsin, Pennsylvania, West Virginia, and here at home in Illinois. As member of a small group of theologian-endorsers, my view has been that expressed by Princeton University professor Cornell West: "I will be your strong advocate until you walk into *Maison Blanc,* then I will be your fiercest critic." I have been troubleshooter in the Jeremiah Wright flap mainly because my students—including Jeremiah's wife, Ramah—serve as assistants at Wright's church, Trinity UCC. During this quite thrilling endeavor, I have been most taken by the promise and possibility of a new politics.

Obama will attempt to end the "old politics" of partisanship, secrecy, passive-aggressive disengagement in the vital things (*e.g.,* Katrina, Israel/

2. Holst, "In the Bleak Midwinter."

3. Vaux, "The Theology of the Presidential Candidates" (available from ken-vaux @garrett.edu).

Palestine, economic regulation) and profuse misengagement in the wrong things (*e.g.*, Iraq, torture, denial of gay rights, fighting "radical Islam"). Fortunately for the new president, the best things in life are free, goods that money can't buy—not much choice there. Much of our constructive agenda will have to be put on hold—perhaps suspended. But with the "new politics" of reaching across the aisle, bipartisanship, transparency, diversity of views, and active participation at the grass-roots-level of the poor and common people, we have a good chance of succeeding.

What have we noted in the diagnostic (problem analysis, deficiency exposure) and prognostic parts of this study? How might these data help us project and set out on new directions? In the first of three thematic areas, I have discovered that what we need at the level of nations is "peace with justice," not the continuation of national arrogance, security obsession, and hegemony. We further need "global reciprocity," not the continuation of global unilateralism, the quest for empire, and disdain and disinterest in other cultures, faiths, and ways of life. Finally. we discover that we need a "New World Order"—political, economic, and ecological—a restoration of God's good will for the whole world, where all nations contribute their particular gifts to all others and to all life and people within this good earth. We no longer need the continuation of the "New American Agenda" that has shown its true colors to be "bases abroad" and continuation of a ruinous national/international policy, now 60 years old, that our university's Steven Kinzer calls "overthrow."[4]

PEACE WITH JUSTICE

Both our analysis of what has gone wrong as America seeks her way in the world and our dissecting of the underlying causal theology shows that we have too often sought peace apart from justice.

But careful biblical-theological analysis shows that there cannot be peace unless there is justice, and peace is the proper goal of justice. The disjoining and severance of these two biblical principles has had devastating effect on both religion and public policy. From biblical times until now, there are myriad "false prophets" who cry "peace, peace, where there is no peace" (Jer 6.14). It's like standing on the ship-deck declaring "mission-accomplished" when strife has just begun. Accomplished peace is

---

4. Kinzer, *Overthrow*.

"breaking down the dividing wall of hostility" (Eph 2. 16), and it is hard, costly work.

To seek to create tranquility while injustice persists is a sham and pretense. The world and its national governments seek this false peace, stand-off, or *Détente*—today in Israel/Palestine, Africa, among the Muslim nations, and with the poor of the world. Just as domestic relations and reconciliations are doomed to obfuscation and endless animosity if we try to "smooth over" conflict rather than confront and deal with underlying injustice and wrong, so national and international crisis would be well-served by honest exposure, recognition of wrong, repentance, restitution, and new beginnings.

The customary processes of adjudication based on power threats, legal manipulation or "bully" tactics need to yield to those of "truth commissions," reconciliation endeavors, searches for understanding, and processes of collaboration among peoples of all nations, faiths, political persuasions, and ways of life.

The concerted complementary wisdom of the Niebuhr brothers, with the amalgam of realism and pacifism they represent, will serve us well in times such as these. We either live in realism or fantasy. Take the issue of Gaza. We can either continue along the pathways of denial, ideological rigidity, and active violence that we now find in the approaches of Israel, *Hamas* and *Hezbollah* and America—or we can seek truth, honest consideration of issues, and the hard work of achieving justice—the precondition of peace.

Rashid Khalili, the most distinguished and knowledgeable Palestinian scholar in America, recently writes of "What we don't know about Gaza" in *The New York Times* (January 2009). His points are clear and precise: Gaza is now populated by those millions dispossessed of their homes in Ashkelon and other towns where Gaza-rockets now land. Gaza seeks to defend itself from intolerable occupation, invasion, and aggression. Are Israel and America asking that Gaza not defend itself? *Hamas* is the legally elected government of Gaza. The humanitarian crisis—health care, economy, electricity, food, and water—is severe as a result of Israel's blockade. Israel's position that Palestine has no right to defend itself, while Israel, with America's help, possesses overwhelming power (including nuclear power) is unconscionable.

GAZA: A DIFFERENT PERSPECTIVE

Meanwhile the Muslim world, and most of the rest of the world for that matter, support open and honest talks about a two-state solution, dialogue between respected neighbors, mutual commitment to the survival and flourishing of the other. For now, negation and mutual demonizing, lies and exaggerations, ill-will, and apocalyptic fantasies of destruction reign supreme, and all hopes of justice-grounded peace go unfulfilled. A different view is expressed in a memo I've just received from the Pastor of Christmas Lutheran Church and College in Bethlehem, Rev. Dr. Mitri Raheb:

> Watching the news these days is not an easy task, especially if you switch between Arab channels like *Al Jazeera* on one hand, and Western channels like Fox on the other. The same conflict is portrayed so differently that one sometimes might wonder if these diverse narratives are actually dealing with the same conflict. On one channel, you see images of children slaughtered by Israeli troops and missiles; on the other, the main story is the rockets launched by *Hamas* into Israel. The most deceiving thing about coverage on both sides, however, is the idea that the more pictures one sees, the more he or she understands what's going on. I believe that the outrageous pictures transmitted are capturing our attention and feelings, yet preventing from thinking, analyzing and understanding what is really happening. This war on Gaza, and the sensational, 24-hour media coverage it is getting, has created a storm in the public sphere in order to hide the real intentions of the parties involved. The most important thing, I believe, is not what we are told and shown, but what this war is trying to hide. Here are some of the intentions as I see them:
>
> *1. The two-state solution is the intended victim of the war on Gaza.*
> Although Israel is aiming at abolishing *Hamas* military capabilities (as primitive as they are), I believe that Israel's real intention is to polish *Hamas'* political image. This may seem an outlandish contradiction, but let's look at what has been happening. While Israel can't tolerate rockets falling into its territory, it is in its long term strategic interest to have *Hamas* control the Gaza Strip. Why? For a simple reason: if *Hamas* controls Gaza and *Fatah* controls the West Bank, then the two-state solution is over. Gaza and the West Bank will become two distinct entities governed by two different Palestinian parties with two different regional alignments. And Israel is off the hook. The "Two-State Solution" that

the Palestinian negotiators were wishfully thinking to have almost achieved in their negotiations with Israel, and what President Bush had promised to deliver by the end of 2008 and didn't, is what was really targeted in this war and totally destroyed. President Obama will find new realities and challenges on the ground to deal with. A new chapter of managing the conflict will start in the Middle East.

2.Regional power struggles continue to be played out in Palestine.

The war on Gaza, although purely an Israeli decision, was also triggered also by some regional powers who were backing *Hamas*. Again we see the same old story played out, of regional wars being fought on Palestinian land, using Palestinian groups and war lords as proxies for different political interests. Without a new regional arrangement, there will be no stability in Palestine or in the region at large.

3.Gaza is the new poster-child for justifying humanitarian aid.

Gaza will now be marketed on a much wider scale as a severe humanitarian crisis. Disempowering aid, handouts, and food supplies will start flowing into Gaza like never before. Yet, Gaza's problem is, fundamentally, a political one. What the people in Gaza really need is for the occupation to end, for the population to be able to live freely, to export and import, to fish and grow flowers. What Gaza really needs is self-empowerment, a new vision, and the power of a spirit that overcomes the liturgies of death and insists on having life that is worth living; even if outside forces deny them that.

Some might ask: Is this the time for such words? People are struggling for mere survival, and you try to talk about things that might be interesting, but not crucial. I disagree. I still remember the days in 2002 when we experienced in Bethlehem the same kind of bombardment with the same F-16s and Apache helicopters (though on a smaller scale and for a much shorter period), when we saw our city that had just been renovated for the millennium celebrations damaged and destroyed. I know how children in Gaza are now being traumatized, how families are scared to death, not knowing who's next. And yet it was at that time that we wrote: "We will never give up on our town and on the wellness of our community. We will continue to build and rebuild, to train and educate, to empower and to create life in the midst of death. We will continue to call for justice and reconciliation in the midst of rising hate, revenge, and retaliation." This was as true then as it is now.[5]

5. Mitri Raheb, "Gaza: A Different Perspective," January 12, 2009.

Today Hillary Clinton is grilled by the Senate Foreign Relations Committee as Secretary of State designate, and Tony Blair receives the highest peace award of this country. In my view, these promising geopolitical developments are highlighted by *realpolitik* and by theopolitics. Tony Blair is the special legate of the Quartet: Europe, America, Russia, and the UN—to mediate peace with justice in the Middle East. In his portfolio is the most promising card of all: his recent religious conversion and his interfaith credentials. With prayer and a heavy dose of faith and love, we may cautiously hope that both the form and substance of justice-grounded peace may gracefully draw near.

The Godness of God

The theological groundwork of this inextricable connection of justice with peace is the nature of God. Righteousness is the character of God. This is not the medieval error of confusing an attribute or accident—justice in this case—with God's self. Rather this assertion recognizes that God, in whom alone truth, good and peace ultimately inheres, also validates justice as that virtue arising in the human being. Justice therefore is the transference into humanity of the peace of divinity.

All peace is of God (Isa 45.7), and only where God is do we find *shalom*. Where peace is, God is. Righteousness (Godness/goodness) is the precondition of peace. In this radical and profound truth, humans hold God's gift of power to bring God and peace into play, through their righteousness by God's grace (Luther). In Psalms 72.7 and 85.10–11, the God who "speaks peace" to the nations enfolds that irenic gift in the actions of persons—Jimmy Carter at Camp David, Secretary-General Ban Ki-moon today in Gaza and in the city of peace—Jerusalem. The "embrace and kiss" is nothing less than the overture and measure of God. Peace of divinity appears through the justice of humanity.

My colleague K. K. Yeo has composed the following prayer for a group of seminary students who had just completed a two-week seminar in Israel and Palestine.

Prayer for Your Humanity, Our Divinity

Gracious God,
Have mercy on us
When our hearts turn cold,

When war and injustice are so common that they trouble us no
more,
When we think Israelis cannot co-exist with Palestinians in the city
of peace.

Have mercy on us
When we think we are religious by loving you without loving our
neighbors,
When we treat neighbors as burdens and respect colleagues only
dutifully,
When we turn cynical because of the haunting past and overwhelming now.

Have mercy on us
When we have sight but no vision,
When fear paralyzes and hope is utopia,
When the cross does not shake us,
The crucifixion no more a stigma,
The resurrection a myth.

Gracious God,
May your faith be our righteousness,
Your hope our vision,
Your love our doxology,
Your image our humanness (as community)
And your humanity, our divinity,
Through Christ our Lord, Amen![6]

Global Reciprocity

Isolation and Hegemony

Our fine-grained analysis of the crisis in the life of nations and America's
role for better or worse has shown that both the decision for isolation
and for hegemony is destructive to others and ourselves, and it is fed by
a disordered theology that heightens both inordinate trust in one's own
superiority and apocalyptic disdain for other peoples. Empire and Evil
Empire are the conjoined symptoms of a diseased theology.

Isolation, even torture, is the opposite of reciprocity as murder is
the opposite of baptism.[7] The cage of Gaza, incarcerating these oppressed

6. Yeo, "Your Humanity, Our Divinity."
7. Prejean, *Dead Man Walking*, 108.

people, exhibits both the pathology and the required therapy I address as I layer in a theology of "a new politics." Pastor Mitri Raheb in his correspondence clearly diagnoses the international chicanery at work in the victimization of Gaza and offers some directions of proposed healing.

THE ABRAHAMIC COVENANT

The theology of politics derivative of the biblical tradition begins with the Abrahamic heritage that sets forth a covenant of the God of history with the polis of the world—a covenant of promise and fulfillment. In Genesis 11, we find a world in fragile coherence and unity of language and purpose after the chaos of Cain and Abel, the antediluvian flood and the proto-covenant of a newly cleansed world with Noah and his family—along with the entourage of rescued creation. In this mythic moment of scripture, human kind and all creation is given to understand that it is known and loved in all its tottering devotion and moral ambiguity by a God who creates, forgives, and keeps on with us in covenant.

Now in Genesis 12, we shift into history as Abram receives the covenantal promise that as he is prepared to move out in trust and justice toward that envisioned land and city that has foundations "whose builder and maker is God" (Heb 11.9), God is prepared to bless him in that great reciprocity with covenanted humanity where he will, in turn, become blessing to the "whole earth." Abraham's identity and destiny is global, not provincial. He is the progenitor in faith and ethics of the Abrahamic families of faith and ethical righteousness (children of *Torah/Tarut*), whose numbers now constitute three-quarters of the world's people and span the globe. These multitudinous faithful will one day be "as the sands of the seas and stars of the skies"(Gen 22.17).

THE NEW COVENANT OF NATIONS

The Abrahamic covenant progresses into the sublime and sad mystery of Reform/Diaspora/*Shoah*/Zion Judaism, and the global faith movements of Christianity and Islam to that Mother Israel has given soul and substance. The covenant of nations now becomes Luke's messianic vision captured from Paul's sermon at Mars hill—the epicenter of an extrabiblical naturalistic world view and philosophy—one that will forever grace the world with a rationalistic companion to faith and ethics. Here Plotinus and Dionysius, Avicenna, Maimonides, and Thomas Aquinas will resort to supply and apply the worldview and way of life they give to the world from the twin towers of reason and revelation.

> . . . People of Athens, I perceive that you are very pious in all things . . . that unknown god you worship, I wish to tell you about. God, who made the world and everything in it . . . doesn't need temples and statues, for He is the *Kurios*/Creator of heaven and earth who gives life and breath to all creatures. He made of the same blood all nations to dwell all over the earth . . . determining the times and places of their habitation, in order that all should seek Him and find Him, for He is very near us and in Him we live, move and have our being . . . (Acts 17.22–28).

The political elements of a theology of nations we can now assert from our deconstruction and reconstruction traces the following lines:

- The world exists for worship ("the world is the theater of God's glory").[8]
- God is known and celebrated in the reciprocity of earth's peoples.
- Worldly "worthship" is defiance that transcends human ambiguity (deciding not to harm those who have harmed you).
- The Abraham project is to venture into life in this world in faith and faith-generated justice.
- In the 2007 document, "A Common Word Between Us and You," the world Muslim community addresses the world Christian community. The preface of their message says, "Without peace and justice between these two religious communities, there can be no meaningful peace in the world. The future of the world depends on peace between Muslims and Christians. The basis of this peace . . . is love of the One God, and (therein) love of the neighbor."[9]

---

8. "For our salvation was a matter of concern to God in such a way that, not forgetful of himself, he kept his glory primarily in view, and therefore, created the whole world for this end, that it may be a theater of his glory," Calvin, *Consensus Genevensis* CO8.294.

9. "A Common Word Between Us and You," A Common Word Web Site, October 13, 2007, www.acommonword.com/lib/downloads/CW-Total-Final-v-12g-Eng-9-10-07.pdf.

A New World Order

Positive Directions

A newer world has already begun to be born. The new creation announced in Romans 8— "... the creature will be released from bondage to the new freedom of the children of God"—is coming. This new exodus is spirited in dynamism but concrete in substance. The one faith of the One God already is growing in the world. Judaism's small beginning and marturial witness now radiates through its own ambiguous Zion and through her children of God—*Akedic* children—Isaac, Ishmael, Jeshua Nazarite—into all the world.

In recent centuries, we witness the preliminaries of a New World Order. The laws of the seas (however unenforced), The United Nations (however flawed), the global economy (however shaky) have emerged in the futility-averting hope (Rom 8) even now gripping the world, straining to be born. Dorothy Jones, Macarthur Fellow and Research scholar at the Newberry Library, has documented the development of this New World Order in her recent book.[10]

Jones argues that an ethical framework has already been developed and is firmly in place in the world that commits the community of nations to peace. This ethical complex—a cumulative body of principles, laws, policies, and programs has been assiduously formulated and then adopted by most nations (often rejected by the "go-it-alone" U.S.). The disdain for the United Nations by the U.S. and Israel, reflected in the bombing of UN headquarters and a school in Gaza, is a significant reservation to Jones' thesis.

Her case proceeds as she unfolds developments in four areas in international life:

- measures of conflict resolution and control;
- standards of social justice;
- human rights guarantees; and
- fundamental principles of international rights.

In hundreds of initiatives these principles, policies, and programs have been introduced and implemented. Today as Eric Holder seeks confirmation as Obama's Attorney-General, the nation ponders and discusses the Geneva Conventions, "water boarding" and torture, and the broader

---

10. See Jones, *Code of Peace*.

system of international norms, the importance of this cache of values vis-à-vis peace and ethics becomes clear.

The ultimate theological ground of any New World Order is not the UN or World Bank or even any version of earthly utopia. Biblical faith from cover to cover—Edenic paradise to the new creation of the Book of Revelation—is about a very special place and time. This state of affairs and order of life is often called the "kingdom of God," "kingdom of Heaven," "realm of God or Christ." It is an etiological and eschatological reality at one level—having to do with how things were made to be or, what they "should" be, or what they one day will be. As we have noted with reference to justice and peace, the reality of New World Order ultimately resides in and is defined by the reality of God in both God's being and attributes. That God "is" justice, love, peace, goodness, mercy, bread, water, life, and the like—up to 100 "qualities" of Divinity in Islam—is of fundamental importance for the kind of concrete New World Order we seek to strive for, work for, and actually lay down in the societies and world order available during our charge.

In sum, the new politics we seek is grounded in a theology that prompts us to seek peace with justice, global reciprocity, and a New World Order. This theological commitment will lead us to have reservations about American bases around the world, American exceptionalism and the new "American Agenda." It will call for the end of theologically based imperialism and hegemony and will seek more salutary understandings of what it might mean to be a chosen people. This latter engagement with public theology and public policy will be especially crucial, given the thoughts I have offered on the Americo-Israeli coalition and collaboration in world history.

The positive directions that arise from these prophetic negations would be:

- Seek to intertwine measures of justice with all endeavors in peace-making.

- Seek to inform all globalization activities with interfaith religious awareness along with the ethical stipulates of all faiths.

- Seek to join dialogue from the faith traditions with discussions of pending world order.

- Seek to curtail American ambitions to create military installations everywhere in the world and rather join with all other nations in making security arrangements for the benefit of every nation.

- Seek to temper belief about American exceptionalism with the belief that all nations have special gifts and that the sharing of these resources for the benefit of all—especially women, children, the elderly, sick and poor—is desirable policy.

- Seek to inform those who think about and plan the American agenda to give central place to theological and ethical values as we formulate our future. The main pertinent theological truths contend that national patriotic values are praiseworthy as are the values of international understanding and cooperation. Nations and international bodies ought to be guided by philosophical principles, laws and religious principles—all guided by the great transcending values of scripture and tradition widely conceived.

- Seek to offer critique of imperialism and hegemony as not in keeping with religious and ethical values. Seek to transform the visions and values of our nation toward affirmation, respect, and helpfulness of all peoples in all nations. Our nation, and all nations, are called to offer their gifts to the world in the times and places given by the God of every nation and the whole world to our nation as well as to others.

- Evil and wrong must be resisted, though we are not to judge others until we have first judged ourselves. The rules of "Just War" are finely tuned axioms by which we can firmly counter attacks and condemn the invasion and occupation of foreign states. There are morally legitimate grounds and means to defend the homeland without resorting to the excesses of the "security state" that forgets rights and sucks up the entire national budget—away from true needs like welfare, education, foreign aid, and health care while it becomes aggressively hegemonic.

FAREWELL OF PRESIDENT BUSH

"Good and evil are present in the world and between the two there can be no compromise." Failing the biblical and Niebuhrian theological principle of first judging ourselves before we judge others—"failing to see the log in our own eye when we see the speck in the other's eye" (Matt 7.1–3)—the President remains stubbornly Manichaean.

The battles waged by our troops are part of a broader struggle between two dramatically different systems. Under one a small band of fanatics demands total obedience to an oppressive ideology, condemns women to subservience, and marks unbelievers for murder. The other system is based on the conviction that freedom is the universal gift of Almighty God and that liberty and justice light the path to peace.[11]

Like the peace and freedom of Iraq and Gaza? The Manichaean worldview, though satisfying to the self-righteous and vindictive, is sub-biblical. The world is not divided into black and white—good guys and bad guys. God alone is good—even Jesus demurs: "Why do you call me good?" (Matt 17.10).With righteousness positioned only in God, the human family is free for a reciprocity of common awareness that we "all have sinned and fallen short" (Rom 3.23), that we need each other and that we all stand weak, finite, and fallible before God. Within this theology, humanity can be bound together as individuals, families, clans, corporations, and nations to effect mutual help, forgiveness, and common tasks.

ECONOMY

A New Global Economy

Human Responsibility

In our analysis of the global economic crisis precipitated by the U.S. and our exposé of the underlying theology that caused that crisis, we found that in addition to the causes of the limited and refracted knowledge, (all that is available in human knowledge of complex, ever-evolving mega-systems), there is the human responsibility of what we do indeed know and can do something about. Because of a deficient moral theology, even today factors like stupidity, injustice, greed, and exploitation of the poor, continue. The ever-present swindlers who swarm toward the vulnerable old, uneducated, and poor in hard times—mostly the smooth talking thieves in big offices and wearing nice suits (as Luther would say)—are alive and well, even as this country seeks to rescue those who suffer under unpayable mortgages and debt. While bankers, lawyers, and loan-sharks

11. George W. Bush, Farewell Address, CBS News, January 18, 2009.

prosper, the poor suffer unemployment, unaffordable health care, deficient education, and a disappearing public and parish safety-net.

This "wanting" theology, we have shown, flirts with following heresies: Radical Religion, The Invisible Hand, and Hoarding the Wealth. Picking up on Kevin Phillips' depiction of what he calls "Radical Religion" that in truth is neither radical nor religion, we can describe the Christian-right Zionism that inspires, in part—as I contend—the crisis in Gaza and in the Middle East.

My acquaintance with Israeli nationals—Ashkenazi, Shephardic, Russian and German—and even the American, Jewish, academic community that has rallied so uncritically to the side of belligerent Israel—does not lead me to find in them the fatal flaws of theology that we find in Bush's farewell. To mention two themes: demonization of the enemy as "radical, militant Islam" (which Bush or his speech-writer may have mercifully dropped) and the exultation of chosen, exceptional people who will be "raptured" in the coming countdown to Armageddon while all others are "left behind." In some calculations, countdown begins in 1948. One does not find these theological notions on the streets of Tel Aviv or Jewish Jerusalem or even on lower-East side New York City. These dispensational-Manichaean ideas are most pronounced in the American Christian Right and to a lesser-extent in the broader evangelical community.[12]

Just as these beliefs are exaggerations of the legitimate doctrines of biblical right and wrong—blessed and cursed behavior—and of the coming and coming back of Jesus Messiah—so the proposed redirection of our national and international life toward a new theology will emphasize the renaissance of critical ethical theology where intense love of God and justice toward the poor and weak compound to renew the world in God's image and intention. Rectifying the economic crisis will not be helped by restoring the conventional and culturated religiosity as we cleanse the more bizarre and idiosyncratic American fundamentalisms. For times such as these, we need insightful and incisive new formulations and pieties.

Casting out the "baby with the bath" in our rejection of Invisible Hand theology will only keep us in the pit of despair and pecuniary

---

12. As mentioned in Part One, dispensationalists support the restoration of Israel as part of the Old Testament promise. The inherent danger in this theology is the identification of final events with the 1948 founding of Israel and a propensity to take violent action against those thought to be the "left-behind" (*e.g.*, American Indians in New England or Muslims in Gaza).

meanness. We will need an imaginative new discovery of the providence of a resplendent and bountiful God and the derivative human confidence and serenity that can respond to others—especially those in acute suffering—in justice and provision. In a speech at a wind-power technology center in Ohio, Barack Obama asked for this kind of theologically realistic risk-taking, hopefulness for the sake of a renewed economy and ecology:

> The need for us to act is now. It's never been more (urgent). We started this year in the midst of a crisis unlike any that we've seen in our lifetime. Last month, we lost more than half a million jobs—a total of almost 2.6 million in 2008. Another 3.4 million people who want and need full-time work have had to settle for part-time jobs.
>
> With each passing day, families here in Ohio and across America are watching their bills pile up and their savings disappear. And economists from across the political spectrum tell us that if nothing is done and we continue on our current path, this recession could linger for years, and America could lose the competitive edge that has served as the foundation for our strength and our standing in the world.
>
> Now, it's not too late to change course, but only if we take dramatic action as soon as possible. The way I see it, the first job of my administration is to put people back to work and get our economy moving again. That's why I've moved quickly to work with my economic team and leaders of both parties on an American recovery and reinvestment plan that will immediate jump start job creation and long-term growth. And I'm pleased that Congress has seen the urgency as well and is moving quickly to consider such a plan.
>
> It's a plan that will create or save 3 million to 4 million jobs in businesses large and small across a wide range of industries. And 90 percent of these jobs will be in the private sector.
>
> I want to be clear: We're not looking to create just any kind of jobs here; we're looking to create good jobs that pay well and can't be shipped overseas; jobs that don't just put people in the short-term, but position our economy to be on the cutting edge in the long- term. And that starts with new, clean sources of energy.
>
> We know that the possibilities are limitless. Here in Ohio and all across America, we've seen old factories become clean energy producers. We've seen entrepreneurs turning solar energy into electricity and corn and soybeans into biofuels.
>
> Our scientists and engineers are hard at work developing cars that use less gas, homes and appliances that require less energy,

schools and offices that are greener and more efficient than ever before.

But we also know that nowhere—nowhere in America are we near realizing the full potential of this work.

Take the example of wind power. We've got representatives from the biggest wind power companies in America here, all who flew in on a day's notice, because they recognize the importance of this moment.

If we don't act now, because of the economic downturn, half of the wind projects planned for 2009 could end up being abandoned. Credit markets have frozen up. It's very difficult because of the capital intensive nature of these projects for them to move forward if they can't get loans, if they can't get access to credit.

And think about that. Think about all the businesses that wouldn't come to be, all the jobs that wouldn't be created, all the clean energy that we wouldn't produce. And think of what's happening in countries like Spain, Germany, and Japan, where they're making real investments in renewable energy. They're surging ahead of us, poised to take the lead in this new industry.

This isn't because they're smarter than us, or work harder than us, or are more innovative than we are. It's because their governments have harnessed their people's hard work and ingenuity with bold investments—investments that are paying off in good, high-wage jobs—jobs they won't lose to other countries.

There's no reason we can't do the same thing right here in America. And that's why, as part of our recovery and reinvestment plan, we are committing to double the production of renewable energy in the next three years, and to modernize more than 75 percent of federal buildings and improve the energy efficiency of 2 million American homes.

That will put people to work. It will save us on our energy bills. It will free us from dependence on foreign oil. In the process, we'll put nearly half a million people to work building wind turbines and solar panels; constructing fuel-efficient cars and buildings; developing the new energy technologies that will lead to new jobs, more savings, and a cleaner, safer planet in the bargain.

That could mean going from operating at 50 percent capacity to 90 percent capacity and creating even more good, made-in-America jobs right here in Ohio.

With our recovery and reinvestment plan, we'll also create hundreds of thousands of jobs by improving health care—transitioning to a nationwide system of computerized medical records that won't just save money, but save lives by preventing deadly medical errors.

And we'll create hundreds of thousands more jobs in educating, equipping tens of thousands of schools with twenty-first-century classrooms, labs and computers to help our kids compete with any workers anywhere in the world.

We'll put nearly 400,000 people to work by repairing our infrastructure—our crumbling roads and bridges and schools. And we'll build the new infrastructure we need to succeed in this new century, investing in science and technology, and laying down miles of new broadband lines so that businesses across our nation can compete with their counterparts around the world.

Finally, we won't just create jobs, we'll also provide help to those who've lost theirs. And I was talking to Governor Strickland, obviously, about the enormous strains on the unemployment insurance system and on Medicaid and Medicare that are—that are being placed during this time.

So we're going to provide help to folks who have lost their jobs, to states and families who've been hardest hit by recession.

That means bipartisan extensions of unemployment insurance and health care coverage; a thousand-dollar tax cut for 95 percent of working families; assistance to help states avoid harmful budget cuts in essential services like police and fire and education, health care, day care.

Now, given the magnitude of these challenges, none of this is going to come easy. Recovery is not going to happen overnight. It's likely that, even with the reinvestment package that we're putting forward, even with the measures that we're taking, things could get worse before they get better. I want everybody to be realistic about this.

But if anyone doubts that we can dig ourselves out of this hole, I invite them here to Ohio and look what you've done here.

It hasn't been easy here either. What you've started wasn't without risk. But here at this company, and in this state, and all across the country, the history of America has been to set our sights higher, to look at the future, not to look back.

In an economy that's losing jobs, we're creating them. And they're the kind of jobs that don't just support families and sustain communities, but also help transform our economy, spurring growth not just today, but for decades to come.

That's what we've always done in moments like this. We've looked ahead to the next big idea, that next new breakthrough. We've experimented and we've innovated. And when we've failed, we've picked ourselves up and we've tried again.

And I know that if we can summon that determination and that great American spirit once again, we will meet the challenges of our time and we build a better future for our children.[13]

To Whom Much Is Given

President Obama's Ohio speech has a careful theology embedded between the lines. It is a theology that seeks the righteous transfer of blessing from "those who have too much" to "those who have too little." Calvin, consistent with much Christian and Abrahamic tradition, believed that either exaggeration—"too much" or "too little"—was unhealthy and unbecoming in God's world.[14] Nevertheless, "hypercapitalist" America and the Middle East oil kingdoms have perpetuated such asymmetric distortions into their present prominence in world history. We begin our discussion of this theology with the first part of that equation.

The constructive theology I offer for the consideration of our religious communities and public entities begins with a clause that has a haunting history and impact: "To whom much is given . . ." (Luke 12.48). The context is a servant who has been endowed with certain gifts (resources) and the dreadful moment of accounting when the Lord returns. It is a common motif in Hebrew, Rabbinic, and Christian pedagogy with certain apocalyptic overtones of judgment—salvation or damnation.

Matthew 25—a very early motif with possible Egyptian origins and wide currency in ancient prophetic, didactic and Sophic (Wisdom) discourse—depicts a righteous, fair, and surprisingly omniscient judge before whom every subject or servant must stand. The theological assumptions are these: Every vassal—who in creation is every person and entity, individual and collective—is responsible and accountable. The goods in hand have been loaned and invested and are not possessed.

Like manna in the wilderness, this is graceful unmerited provision from God, who hears the cry of distress, to those in need—given through "the established work of our hands" (Psa 90.17)—those able-bodied to "earn, save and give" (Wesley). The resourcefulness of these provisions have not been earned and they are not "possessed." We can turn them into gifts to the "least of these" or contort them into hoarded "mammon."(Matt 6.19). In Matthew 25, our immediate and ultimate well being is deter-

13. Barack Obama, Speech at Cardinal Fastener, January 16, 2009, Bedford Heights, Ohio.

14. See John Calvin's commentary on 2 Corinthians 8, *New Testament Commentaries*.

mined by our choices in the face of that awesome "to whom much" . . . and whether we "clothed the naked . . ." with the largesse we enjoyed.

The parable in its ancient setting pertains to public officials and representatives of the people. In the ancient near-east and elsewhere, the human community is a corporeal solidarity with officials, even kings who are representatives and participants in divinity but also responsible to the common people. The economic parable, in other words, seals the inextricable connection of divinity and humanity—of sacred and secular duty.

At a baccalaureate meditation at Stanford University in 1996, Rev. Dr. J. Alfred Smith, Sr. pondered this passage: "For unto whomsoever much is given, of him shall be much required" (Luke 12.48). Citing an incident with a group of children in Sierra Leone, Rev. Smith recalled his realization that "Americans are a people to whom much is given." He reminded graduates that, while the U.S. has only six percent of the world's total population, it uses "one-third of the earth's non-renewable resources and one-fourth of the gross planetary production of goods and services." Smith asked graduates, "Will you balance your need for earning enough compensation to pay off your academic bills with a commitment to the community?" and he encouraged them to consider whether they, "who have been given much, will contribute to the unity that can exist in human community."[15]

Striking Kierkegaard's "Right Note,"[16] sounded in the song of praise to God and kindness to others rising from the voice even of one who is hurting, is like a symphony of justice, grace, and love drowning out the cacophony of greed, opportunism, and ingratitude in the world's awful dirge.

Responding to this great commission of mission, "To whom much is given," Albert Schweitzer proposed that every medical student in his homeland of France be expected to offer a period of "return service"—in his case, to the sick and suffering of Africa—in obligatory but welcomed gratitude for the society that had provided his or her education. This proposal was a parable on our theological couplet. Such proposals of publicly funded national and international service will be an essential part, we can hope of Obama's stimulus plan. As Obama himself remarked in many campaign speeches, "we must care and not suffer empathy deficit."

---

15. J. Alfred Smith, Sr., Baccalaureate Address, June 15, 1996, Stanford University, Palo Alto, California, Stanford University News Service Press Release, issued June 17, 1996, www.stanfordu.edu/dept/news/pr/96/960617smithbacc.html.

16. See Dru, *The Journals of Søren Kierkegaard.*

To the Least of These

The receiving pole of the equation of our new theology defines our obligations and opportunities of justice and generosity. God has ordered and assembled the world good and provident—abundant and fulsome—if resources are artfully received and shared. "He opens His hand and satisfies the desire of every living thing" (Psa 145.16). Plenitude and all-sufficiency is the first and last word of scripture in the Abrahamic and all faiths. But there is another dark and ambiguous side. This is the enigma addressed by Calvin when he speaks of the "mystery of the rich and poor" or Jesus' so often mischievously-misinterpreted words, "You will always have the poor with you" (Matt 26.11). Though Jesus' words accent the juxtaposition of our not having Himself with us for long but having the poor forever—the fact remains that a large sector of the world's population has always been poor and may always be so.

"The least of these" also comes from the signature parable already cited in Matthew 25— "Inasmuch as you have done/not done this to the least of these my brothers you have done/not done it to me" (Matt 25.40, 45). This monumental text called "the parable of the sheep and goats" or "Parable of the Nations," is of signal importance to my thesis.

I highlight several references to the phrase in Obama's speeches. In a conversation with Pastor Rick Warren at Saddleback Church in Lake Forest, California, he spoke of two themes related to the "least of these": 1) Commitment and action on behalf of the least of these is the decisive criterion of whether this is a "nation under God," and 2) Our commitment to the poor is expressed in the "merciful works" signaled by this parable and by the watchword phrase.

On the occasion of a trip to New Orleans with former President Bill Clinton (September 6, 2005) during the aftermath of the debacle of national response to Hurricane Katrina, Obama admonished, "our poor Americans—mostly black—must be fed, clothed, housed, and provided the medical care they need. We need to stabilize the situation now and into the future." Then, speaking of the public-policy scandal of dikes and levees that made the marsh-land areas highly vulnerable, he spoke of preventing future disasters. He cited the embarrassing spectacle to the world: the wealthy in their SUVs, filling their tanks with $100 worth of gasoline and high-tailing it out of town to safety, while poor African-American residents huddled in the Superdome or shakily trembled on the ramshackle roofs of their homes. His final words in New Orleans were sobering: "I'm afraid that I see only continuation (of neglect) and the failure of government toward 'the least of these.'"[17] Now that he is President, we may hope that our nation and others will avert the parable's judgment on the poor goats on the left and move to the side of the sheep on the right.

Obama gave a lengthy reflection on the matter in his speech on "Faith-Based Organizations" at Zanesville, Ohio. The passage is obviously on his mind as he speaks:

> You know, faith based groups like East Side Community Ministry carry a particular meaning for me. Because in a way, they're what led me into public service. It was a Catholic group called The Campaign for Human Development that helped fund the work I did many years ago in Chicago to help lift up neighborhoods that were devastated by the closure of a local steel plant.
>
> Now, I didn't grow up in a particularly religious household. But my experience in Chicago showed me how faith and values could be an anchor in my life. And in time, I came to see my faith as being both a personal commitment to Christ and a commitment to my community; that while I could sit in church and pray all I want, I wouldn't be fulfilling God's will unless I went out and did the Lord's work.
>
> There are millions of Americans who share a similar view of their faith, who feel they have an obligation to help others. And they're making a difference in communities all across this country—through initiatives like Ready4Work, which is helping ensure that ex-offenders don't return to a life of crime; or Catholic Charities, which is feeding the hungry and making sure we don't have homeless veterans sleeping on the streets of Chicago; or the good work that's being done by a coalition of religious groups to rebuild New Orleans.
>
> You see, while these groups are often made up of folks who've come together around a common faith, they're usually working to help people of all faiths or of no faith at all. And they're particularly well-placed to offer help. As I've said many times, I believe that change comes not from the top-down, but from the bottom-up, and few are closer to the people than our churches, synagogues, temples, and mosques.
>
> I'm not saying that faith-based groups are an alternative to government or secular nonprofits. And I'm not saying that they're

---

17. Barack Obama, Statement on Hurricane Katrina Relief Efforts, September 6, 2005, New Orleans, Louisiana.

somehow better at lifting people up. What I'm saying is that we all have to work together—Christian and Jew, Hindu and Muslim, believer and non-believer alike—to meet the challenges of the twenty-first century.

Now, I know there are some who bristle at the notion that faith has a place in the public square. But the fact is, leaders in both parties have recognized the value of a partnership between the White House and faith-based groups. President Clinton signed legislation that opened the door for faith-based groups to play a role in a number of areas, including helping people move from welfare to work. Al Gore proposed a partnership between Washington and faith-based groups to provide more support for "the least of these." And President Bush came into office with a promise to "rally the armies of compassion," establishing a new Office of Faith-Based and Community Initiatives.

But what we saw instead was that the Office never fulfilled its promise. Support for social services to the poor and the needy have been consistently underfunded. Rather than promoting the cause of all faith-based organizations, former officials in the Office have described how it was used to promote partisan interests. As a result, the smaller congregations and community groups that were supposed to be empowered ended up getting short-changed.

With these principles as a guide, my Council for Faith-Based and Neighborhood Partnerships will strengthen faith-based groups by making sure they know the opportunities open to them to build on their good works. Too often, faith-based groups—especially smaller congregations and those that aren't well connected—don't know how to apply for federal dollars, or how to navigate a government Website to see what grants are available, or how to comply with federal laws and regulations. We rely too much on conferences in Washington, instead of getting technical assistance to the people who need it on the ground. What this means is that what's stopping many faith-based groups from helping struggling families is simply a lack of knowledge about how the system works.

Well, that will change when I'm president. I will empower the nonprofit religious and community groups that do understand how this process works to train the thousands of groups that don't. We'll "train the trainers" by giving larger faith-based partners like Catholic Charities and Lutheran Services and secular nonprofits like Public/Private Ventures the support they need to help other groups build and run effective programs. Every house of worship that wants to run an effective program and that's willing to abide by our constitution—from the largest mega-churches and synagogues to the smallest store-front churches and mosques—can and will have access to the information and support they need to run that program.

This Council will also help target our efforts to meet key challenges like education. All across America, too many children simply can't read or perform math at their grade-level, a problem that grows worse for low-income students during the summer months and after school hours. Nonprofits like Children's Defense Fund are working to solve this problem. They hold summer and after school Freedom Schools in communities across this country, and many of their classes are held in churches. There's a lot of evidence that these kinds of partnerships work. Take "Youth Education for Tomorrow," an innovative program that's being run by churches, faith-based schools, and others in Philadelphia. To help narrow the summer learning gap, the YET program hires qualified teachers who help students with reading using proven learning techniques. They hold classes four days a week after school and during the summer. And they monitor progress closely. The results have been outstanding. Children who attended a YET center for at least six months improved nearly two years in reading ability. And the average high school student gained a full grade in reading level after just three months.

That's the kind of real progress that can be made when we empower faith-based organizations. And that's why as president, I'll expand summer programs like this to serve one million students. This won't just help our children learn, it will help keep them off the streets during the summer so they don't turn to crime.

And my Council for Faith-Based and Neighborhood Partnerships will also have a broader role—it will help set our national agenda. Because if we are going to do something about the injustice of millions of children living in extreme poverty, we need interfaith coalitions like the "Let Justice Roll Campaign" standing up for the powerless. If we're going to end genocide and stop the scourge of HIV/AIDS, we need people of faith on Capitol Hill talking about how these challenges don't just represent a security crisis or a humanitarian crisis, but a moral crisis as well.

We know that faith and values can be a source of strength in our own lives. That's what it's been to me. And that's what it is to so many Americans. But it can also be something more. It can be the foundation of a new project of American renewal. And that's the kind of effort I intend to lead as president of the United States.[18]

The new theology we draw on is actually quite old. There is no postmodern twist to the universal narrative we have invoked. That the love of

18. Barack Obama, Remarks at East Side Community Ministry, July 1, 2008, Zanesville, Ohio.

God is realized in human ethics is the perennial wisdom of all religion and philosophy. As such, it lends itself to translation into public policy in the pluralistic and interfaith context that is our public life. The couplet of national commitment to human welfare out of our received bounty to those in our midst and in every corner of the world—is the compound charter of economic theology that we commend to our nation and the world.

ECOLOGY

A New Ecology

SIMPLICITY, FRUGALITY, AND SHARING

As President-Elect Obama retraces the train route of Abraham Lincoln from Philadelphia to Washington D.C. for the inauguration of a new era in the life of this nation—the Met Opera of the week is John Adams' Doctor Atomic. So on this bleak midwinter day, the nation throbs with political and theological history. Doctor Atomic addresses "the most emphatic symbol of America's crisis in the world."[19] The story is of physicist Robert Oppenheimer and those who built (and proceeded to test and use) the first nuclear weapons in the history of the world.

The bombing of the Japanese cities—Hiroshima and Nagasaki—precedes the other world-historical event—the founding of the state of Israel by a few short years. The former event affects the history of nature and the latter, the nature of history.

When I was a young graduate student at Princeton, I was invited to the Institute for Advanced Studies for dinner and to present my College Oration that had won a national award the year before. The fellows kindly received the young theologian's aweless words: "Modern Science: Man's Salvation or His Doom." As the evening proceeded, it turned out that my remarks were the hors d'oeuvres before the main course—the Advanced Institute's Director Robert Oppenheimer. "Not a bad double bill," I smugly said to myself, "two brilliant critiques of modern science."

How surprised I was when Oppenheimer spoke on the topic of "Sanskrit Poetry." The brilliant and remorseful scientist/philosopher was already the subject of attacks from "right-wing" fanatics who questioned his patriotism and trumped-up communist associations. But all of us that

19. John Adams, "Doctor Atomic," The Metropolitan Opera, New York, New York.

night and throughout the world have seen his rehabilitation and eventual partnership with Princeton's other wise-man, Albert Einstein, in concerns for world disarmament and peace. We now know that we were in the presence of a conscientious pioneer of this new age.

The theology of creation was at stake on this evening symposium and in the opera. Oppenheimer, the "American Prometheus," spoke on the Hindu Scripture—Bhagavad Gita—and its terrified, penetrating glimpse into God and human prescience and resultant danger. "Brighter than a thousand suns" foretold a cosmic conflagration where all human ingenuity and divine quarantine conjoined in an apocalyptic *denouement* of all nature and history.[20]

THEOLOGIES OF ECOLOGY AND CREATION

I have consulted Walter Brueggemann's biblical theology of the earth for this portion of my indictment and constructive proposal. I also could look at the many thoughtful ecological theologies and theologies of creation. Rosemary Ruether's *Gaia and God* and John Polkinghorne's *Science and Creation* are representative works of these motifs. The common emphases for our purposes from both theologies of the natural reality include:

- attitudes of reverence toward the "good world" of God's creation;

- acceptance of stewardship as our sacred duty; and

- awareness that the world belongs to God with whom we are collaborators in *Tikkun Olam*, the building (Teilhard de Chardin) and repair (Heschel) of the earth.

- The entire world is God's creation and all the people who ever lived on earth or ever will live here inherit its resources and share responsibility for its protection and use.

- Abuse and misuse—from acid rain to global warming, defacing and murderous war in Gaza to carbon footprints that assume that the world ends with this generation—are despicable and must end in this new world.

- The attitudes of earth destruction, end of the world, and lust for apocalypse must be altered toward respect, reverence, and responsibility. Thanksgiving is the response of justice, not living selfishly or hedonistically.

---

20. Bhagavad Gita, ch. 11, v. 12.

- Animals, plants, and all creatures share in the precious nature of creation and deserve any protection we can offer.

- A new theology of life on earth both takes responsibility for the creation and accedes to the mystery of God's providence in the world and His will as arbiter of the beginning and ending of the cosmos. We must believe that everything depends on God and act as everything depends on us.[21]

A cease-fire goes into effect today in Gaza. Will it be an inspiration to the nation gathered in Washington, D.C. for the inauguration? The coincidence with the Martin Luther King, Jr. holiday—reluctantly signed into law by President Ronald Reagan—is uncanny.

Our concluding thoughts focus on a new ecology: simplicity, frugality, and sharing—fitting for a nation and world now moving to a new ascetic from its decades-long shopping and gambling spree.

TABLE THEOLOGY

> Tis a gift to be simple, Tis a gift to be free,
> Tis a gift to come round where we want to be.
> And when we find ourselves in the place just right,
> Twill be in the valley of love and delight.[22]

The best theology I can commend to our nation and through that nation to the world is a simple distillation of the theological wisdom entrusted to the faiths of Father Abraham, mediated by Messiah, Logos, Sophia, *Mahdi*—messengers of divinity to humanity, and animated, spirited and "put to work" in this redemption-starved world by simple, frugal believers—the poor peasants of God's heart.

The Gaza atrocity began to unravel and the preconditions for peace arose when Israel inadvertently bombed UN headquarters in Gaza City while Secretary-General Ban Ki-moon was in town. The Buddhist general (strange oxymoron) decried the injustice and the Israeli commander named, of all things, Barack, calling the action "most regrettable"—probably sealing his loss in upcoming Israeli elections. Still we pray: "*Barack-Atah-Adonai-Elohenu-Melech-Ha-Olam.*"

We need a new theology, one that my good wife Sara calls "table-talk theology." Her work as the world's leading scholar on the work of Clint

---

21. See Ruether, *Gaia and God* and Polkinghorne, *Science and Creation*.

22. Joseph Brackett, Jr., "Simple Gifts," *The Gift To Be Simple: Shaker Rituals and Songs,* 1848.

Eastwood—quintessential American bad guy now transformed into a saintly, reconciled, *Akedic* witness to transformative love that he learns at the resplendent, succulent Hmong table in desperate Detroit—has guided these reflections throughout. Table talk—Eucharistic, Asian, African, Middle-East table on the dirt floor—and table theology—simple, frugal and given to sharing—may be all that can get us through this frightening now.

This theology is the antithesis of the regnant American creed. We have characterized that theology as Triumphalist, Exceptionalist, Manichaeanist, Cheneyist, and Exclusivist. What is called for is a new theology of the world.

Its qualities will be humble and servile, collegial and universal. Rather than seeking to create a "security state" that would seem to be all that is needed to create a "security calamity," Walter Brueggemann and the biblical witness commends, "trust in God" and the "doing of justice" as the best insurance of security. Planning to prevent a cyber-attack would seem to set in motion the very knowledge and technology to make such an attack inevitable. As with Doctor Atomic's forebodings, weapons stores and elaborate preparations of war machines have always been the precursors for the use of such.

Now such wisdom—even the playing of the theological card—may be greeted with skepticism. One political commentator—a frightful breed I've found over these past two weary campaign years—says this morning that what is needed is not divine intervention but government intervention. Reflecting on the Japanese recession of the 1990's, which lasted a decade and caused property values to fall 87 percent, said commentator admonished that we need payers not prayers—"praise the Lord and pass the ammunition." The amazing ditch-landing of the U.S. Air jet this week in the Hudson River certainly was a "coming in on a wing and a prayer."

Ora et Labora—obviously is the answer. Prayer and work is the answer of the ascetic Benedictine tradition. When Barack Obama takes the Presidential oath of office from the Chief Justice of the Supreme Court this week (on the Lincoln Bible), it will be remembered that Obama was one who voted against the Bush nominee in 2005 because, "It is my personal estimation that he has far more often used his formidable skills on behalf of the strong in opposition to the weak."[23] Monastic strength is like

23. Linda Greenhouse, "Two Stars Meeting Across a Bible," *The New York Times*, January 18, 2009.

that of the Christ "made perfect in weakness" (2 Cor 12.9). Weakness that is real strength is like the foolishness that is true wisdom.

A NEW GOD FOR A NEW AGE

Again the heart of any theology relevant to the national life is anchored in the "Reality of God." The spokesman of such a theology that I find most compelling is found in the refreshing texts of the Gods of Hebrew and Christian story developed in the narrative theology of Pulitzer-prize winner Jack Miles.

In *God: A Biography*, Miles explores the paradoxical Big Man hovering in the shadowy background who issues contradictory commands: "Be fruitful and multiply" next to an imposition of circumcision (control on sexuality); of "take your only and beloved son and offer him," but then, "do not lay a hand on the lad" (Gen 22); and if we allow *Rabah midrash*— "Why are you celebrating?" (the drowning of the pursuing Egyptians in the Exodus), "they too are my people" (Exod 15).[24]

In *Christ: A Crisis in the Life of God*, this paradoxical *midrashic* tale starts to morph into a depiction of a contradictory "being." As I develop in *Ethics and the War on Terrorism*, a warrior god is slowly transformed into one more silent and non-violent because holy war hasn't and doesn't work—if it ever did. The "new" or "newly discovered" God—one more vulnerable and codependent on people—is now being born and setting out on a new kind of life to redeem and renew the world.[25]

Though the history of God superintends economic and political history, tracing this intertwining tale is difficult. Jubilee (Luke 4.19) in the history of Israel, for example, is a pressure valve to release pent-up debt and unjust concentration of wealth and land-holdings. In other words, Jubilee is about buy-back or redemption. Now we may say that economic history is altering the history of God or a transmuting God is rectifying the human distortions of economy.

Miles looks with vivid literary wonder at the phenomenon of Christ—the anointed King who must die, the warrior who must seemingly fall and fail, the defeated One whose defeat is the only viable victory over all defeat. On close inspection, the cross is hidden glory. Miles agonizes over "the improbable and appalling conjunction of expiatory Lamb

---

24. See Miles, *God*.

25. See Miles, *Christ* and Vaux, *Ethics and the War on Terrorism*.

and Messianic War-lord"[26] but *Sub specie aeternitatis*, this is the Hallelujah victory of God over the "powers of the world."

The cross/resurrection, time/space, infinity/eternity event is economic, ecological, and political in its deepest implications. The theological reality conveyed here impinges on all the dimensions of our study. I detail these ramifications in a treatment of Miles' biblical theology in *Ethics and the War on Terrorism*. By reason of the redemption injected into the world by the virtue of Emmanuel God:

- The weight of the injustice and wrong that besets the world is confronted by the ameliorative power of God.

- The inertia and inequity of the world is set askance and therefore made amenable to the movement of the Spirit of God.

- Human responsibility is now rendered efficacious to challenge injustice in systems and to effect salutary change in those same systems and structures.

- We are guided by divine mandate—*i.e.*, "do not steal" from the neighbor, (Lev 19.13), the poor, (Prov 22.22), the widow, (Isa 10.2), and ultimately the "Giver of all"—"Do not rob God" (Mal 3.8). If we allow others and God their "right"—the world (and God) will not turn against us.

HINTS OF CHANGE

The Inaugural texts provide a good summary for my study. Obama's address touches on my themes of economics, power and security, and religion:

> Forty-four Americans have now taken the presidential oath. The words have been spoken during rising tides of prosperity and the still waters of peace. Yet, every so often the oath is taken amidst gathering clouds and raging storms.
>
> Our economy is badly weakened, a consequence of greed and irresponsibility on the part of some but also our collective failure to make hard choices and prepare the nation for a new age.
>
> Homes have been lost, jobs shed, businesses shuttered. Our health care is too costly, our schools fail too many, and each day brings further evidence that the ways we use energy strengthen our adversaries and threaten our planet.

Obama speaks again on the theme of "to whom much is given":

26. Miles, *Christ*, 27.

We remain the most prosperous, powerful nation on earth. Our workers are no less productive, our minds no less inventive, our goods and services no less needed than . . . when this crisis began. Our capacity remains undiminished.

The state of our economy calls for action: bold and swift. And we will act not only to create new jobs but to lay a new foundation for growth. We will build the roads and bridges, the electric grids and digital lines that feed our commerce and bind us together. We will restore science to its rightful place and wield technology's wonders to raise health care's quality.

Nor is the question before us whether the market is a force for good or ill. Its power to generate wealth and expand freedom is wonderful. But this crisis has reminded us that without a watchful eye, the market can spin out of control—and that a nation cannot prosper long when it favors only the prosperous. The success of our economy has always depended not just on the size of our GDP but the reach of our prosperity; in our ability to extend opportunity to every willing heart—not out of charity, but because it is the surest route to our common good.

To the people of poor nations we pledge to work alongside you to make your farms flourish and let clean water flow; to nourish starved bodies and feed hungry minds.

Obama continues on the themes of power and security:

As for our common defense, we reject the false choice between our safety and our ideals . . . We must not give up the rule of law and human rights—those (values) secured by the blood of generations. Those ideals still light the world and we will not give them for expediency's sake.

Recall that our early generations faced down fascism and communism, not just with missiles and tanks, but with sturdy alliances and enduring convictions. They understood that our power alone cannot protect us nor does it enable us to do as we please. Power grows through its prudent use. Our security emanates from the justness of our cause—the force of our example—the tempering qualities of humility and restraint.

He calls for mutual interest and respect among diverse peoples:

Our patchwork heritage is a strength, not a weakness. We are a nation of Christians, Muslims, Jews and Hindus—and non-believers. To the Muslim world we seek a new way forward based on mutual interest and mutual respect. To those who cling to power through deceit and silencing dissent—we extend a hand if you are unwilling to unclench your fist.[27]

The Inaugural Poem by Elizabeth Alexander echoes these themes:

Praise song for struggle; praise song for the day. Some live by "love thy neighbor as thyself." Others by first do no harm, or take no more than you need. What if the mightiest word is love, love beyond marital, filial, national. Love that casts a widening pool of light. Love with no need to preempt grievance. In today's sharp sparkle, this winter air, anything can be made, any sentence begun. Praise song for walking forward in that light.[28]

HUMOR, HUMUS, AND HUMILITY

Pastor Lowery's benediction brings it all home:

While we have sown the seeds of greed, the wind of greed and corruption, even as we reap the whirlwind of social and economic disruption, we ask for forgiveness and the spirit of unity and solidarity.

Deliver us from the exploitation of the poor, "least of these" and from favoritism toward the rich "elite of these."

We ask you to help us work for that day,

when black will not be asked to get in back,

when brown can stick around,

when yellow will be mellow,

when the red man can get ahead man,

and when white will embrace what is right.[29]

CONCLUSION

I have followed through on my thesis that the present crisis of America's place and activity in God's world has deleterious aspects provoked by underlying deficient theologies. I have probed corrective theologies offered by the best minds on the matters under discussion, and these have supplied my constructive theological proposals. It is now up to all of us to see what can be done to right the course of our beloved nation—in church,

---

27. Barack Obama, Inaugural Address, January 20, 2009, Washington, D.C.

28. Elizabeth Alexander, "Praise Song for the Day: A Poem for Barack Obama's Presidential Inauguration" (Saint Paul, Minn.: Graywolf Press, forthcoming).

29. Joseph Lowery, Inauguration Benediction, January 20, 2009, Washington, D.C.

synagogue and mosque and in the corridors of public life—especially politics, economics, and environment. By God we can do it, Yes we can!

BENEDICTION

I toss and turn as the gentle snow falls. Early news is that Obama's economic stimulus package of nearly $1 trillion comes to vote in the house today, and the debate the new president loves wages among his closest advisors, including the vice president. Shall we start bombing and killing in Afghanistan and Pakistan, or shall we start talking and building? We pray for the latter wisdom. This study laments the recent decade when we have taken the U.S. defense/security budget from $300 billion to nearly $1 trillion, and the edifice of rational and global justice, peace and security has tumbled—along with the global economy. *Tikkum Olam* is shattered.

In Israel, a great wall of security around Jerusalem and Bethlehem—the world's place of peace and house of bread—is out-disgraced only by the Gaza Strip lying in rubble—22,000 homes and buildings destroyed, and thousands of bereaved in mourning, as the burned and wounded receive little medical aid because Isaiah's Highway of Torah is blocked (Isa 40). *Tikkum Olam* is shattered.

But I take hope knowing that, though our sins be as scarlet, they shall be white as snow (Isa 1.18). It is snowy Epiphany-tide in Midwestern American Christendom—snow upon snow—and we ponder the deep midwinter, long ago, and wonder with Yeats:

> Things fall apart; the centre cannot hold . . .
> Mere anarchy is loosed upon the world . . .
> The best lack all conviction, while the worst
> Are full of passionate intensity.
> Surely some revelation is at hand;
> Surely the Second Coming is at hand.
> And what rough beast, its hour come round at last,
> Slouches toward Bethlehem to be born?[30]

Evanston, Illinois
January 2009

---

30. W. B. Yeats, "The Second Coming," *The Golden Treasury of Poetry*, ed. Oscar Williams (Denver: Mentor Books, 1953).

Discussion and Study Guide

1

CRISIS IN THE LAND

1. Is the three-fold program of America's engagement in God's world—Bases abroad, Bad Money, and Black Gold—good or evil?

2. What are the pros and cons of American "exceptionalism"?

3. From the faith perspective, what are the gifts America should bring to God's world?

4. What are the theological and ethical causes of the economic crisis?

5. Is the novel realm of "finance" a) a necessity of economic life in our world today; b) a demonic power robbing the poor; or c) Gandhi's "wealth without work" (the first "blunder" of the world)?

2

CONTOURS OF A DEFICIENT THEOLOGY AND ETHICS

1. What are the theological virtues and vices of empire?

2. What are the "worthy" and "unworthy" meanings of "chosen people?"

3. What are the theological errors of Manichaeanism, the "Invisible Hand," and "Radical Religion?"

3

CREATIVE THEOLOGY
AND THE PROMISE OF A BETTER FUTURE

1. What do the Niebuhr brothers offer to an American theology of nations?

2. Which theology of economics do you prefer: Long, Tanner or Meeks?

3. How would you outline and critique Brueggemann's theology of land?

4

CONSTRUCTIVE THEOLOGICAL
AND ETHICAL DIRECTIONS

1. Sketch your own theology and ethics of nations.
2. Sketch your own theology and ethics of economy.
3. Sketch your own theology and ethics of politics.
4. Sketch your own theology and ethics of environment.

Bibliography

Badiou, Alain. *Metapolitics*, trans. Jason Barker. New York: Verso, 2005.

Becker, Ernest. *The Denial of Death*. New York: Simon & Schuster, Inc., 1973.

Bieler, Andre. *The Social Humanism of Calvin*. Louisville: John Knox Press, 1964.

Bonhoeffer, Dietrich. *Letters and Papers from Prison*. New York: Touchstone, 1997.

Brueggemann, Walter. *Hope Within History*. Atlanta: John Knox Press, 1987.

———. *The Land: Place as Gift, Promise and Challenge in Biblical Faith*. Minneapolis: Augsburg Fortress, 2002.

Brzezinski, Zbigniew and Scowcroft, Brent. *America and the World: Conversations on the Future of American Foreign Policy*. New York: Basic Books, 2008.

Buber, Martin. *On Zion: The History of an Idea*, trans. Stanley Godman. Syracuse: Syracuse University Press, 1997.

Burtt, E.A. *The Metaphysical Foundations of Modern Science*. Mineola, NY: Dover Publications, 2003.

Chesterton, G. K. *The Collected Works of G.K. Chesterton: What I Saw in America, the Resurrection of Rome, and Side Lights*. San Francisco: Ignatius Press, 1990.

Crossan, John Dominic. *God and Empire: Jesus Against Rome, Then and Now*. New York: HarperCollins Publishers, 2007.

Derrida, Jacques. *The Gift of Death*, trans. David Wills. Chicago: University of Chicago Press, 1995.

Eskola, Timo. *Messiah and the Throne: Jewish Merkabah Mysticism and Early Christian Exaltation Discourse*. Philadelphia: Coronet Books, 2001.

Facultés jésuites de Paris. *L'exégèse patristique de Romains 9–11: Grâce et liberté; Israël et nations; Le mystère du Christ*. Paris: Centre Sèvres, 2007.

Ferguson, Niall. *Colossus: The Price of America's Empire*. New York: Penguin Group, 2004.

Fletcher, Joseph. *Moral Responsibility: Situation Ethics At Work*. Norwich, UK: SCM Press, 1967.

Friedman, Milton. *Capitalism and Freedom*. Chicago: University of Chicago Press, 1962/1982/2002.

Gandhi, M. K. "Non-violence—the Greatest Force." *Peace Is the Way: Writings on Nonviolence from the Fellowship of Reconciliation*, ed. Walter Wink. Maryknoll, NY: Orbis Books, 2000.

Gearty, Conor. *Can Human Rights Survive*? Cambridge: Cambridge University Press, 2006.

Gollwitzer, Helmut. *The Rich Christians and Poor Lazarus*. Somerset, UK: St. Andrew's Press, 1970.

Goodman, Martin. *Rome and Jerusalem: The Clash of Ancient Civilizations*. New York: Knopf, 2007.

Greenspan, Alan. *The Age of Turbulence: Adventures in a New World*. New York: The Penguin Group, 2007.

Habermas, Jürgen. *The Divided West*. Cambridge, UK: Polity Press, 2006.

———. "Religion in the Public Sphere," *European Journal of Philosophy* 14: 1–25, J. Gaines (trans.).

Hauerwas, Stanley. *Vision and Virtue: Essays in Christian Ethical Reflection*. Notre Dame, IN: Fides Publishers, 1974.

Horsley, Richard A., ed. *In the Shadow of Empire: Reclaiming the Bible As a History of Faithful Resistance*. Louisville: Westminster John Knox Press, 2008.

Jenkins, Phillip. *God's Continent: Christianity, Islam and Europe's Religious Crisis*. New York: Oxford University Press, 2007.

Jewett, Robert and Lawrence, John. *Captain America and the Crusade Against Evil: The Dilemma of Zealous Nationalism*. Grand Rapids: Eerdmans, 2004.

Jewett, Robert et al. *Romans: A Commentary (Hermeneia: A Critical and Historical Commentary on the Bible*. Minneapolis: Fortress Press, 2006.

Johnson, Chalmers. *The Sorrows of Empire: Militantism, Secrecy, and the End of the Republic*. New York: Henry Holt and Company, LLC, 2004.

Jonas, Hans. "The Burden and Blessing of Mortality." *Bioethics: Basic Writings on the Key Ethical Questions That Surround the Major, Modern Biological Possibilities and Problems*, ed. Thomas A. Shannon. Mahwah, NJ: Paulist Press, 1993.

Jones, Dorothy V. *Code of Peace: Ethics and Security in the World of the Warlord States*. Chicago: University of Chicago Press, 1989.

Kagan, Robert. *The Return of History and the End of Dreams*. New York: Knopf, 2008.

Kinzer, Stephen. *Overthrow: America's Century of Regime Change From Hawaii to Iraq*. New York: Henry Holt & Company, LLC, 2006.

Krugman, Paul R. *The Return of Depression Economics*. New York: W.W. Norton & Company, Inc., 1999/2000.

Levenson, Jon. *The Death and Resurrection of the Beloved Son*. New Haven: Yale University Press, 1995.

———. *Resurrection and the Restoration of Israel: The Ultimate Victory of the God of Life*. New Haven: Yale University Press, 2006.

———. "Resurrection in the Torah: A Second Look" Center for Theological Inquiry, www.ctinquiry.org/publications/reflections_volume_6/levenson.htm.

———. *Sinai and Zion: An Entry Into the Jewish Bible*. New York: HarperOne, 1987.

Lewis, C.S. *Perelandra and That Hideous Strength*. New York: Simon & Schuster, Inc., 1996.

Long, D. Stephen. *Divine Economy: Theology and the Market*. London: Routledge, 2000.

Mailer, Norman. *Of a Fire on the Moon*. New York: Grove Press, 1985.

McCain, John and Salter, Mark. *Hard Call: The Art of Great Decisions*. New York: Hachette Book Group, USA, 2008.

McFague, Sallie. *The Body of God: An Ecological Theology*. Minneapolis: Augsburg Fortress, 1993.

McKibben, Bill. *The End of Nature*. New York: Random House, Inc. 1989/1999.

Meeks, M. Douglas. *God the Economist: The Doctrine of God and Political Economy*. Minneapolis: Augsburg Fortress, 1989.

Migliore, Daniel L. *The Power of God and the Gods of Power*. Louisville: The Westminster John Knox Press, 2008.

Miles, Jack. *Christ: A Crisis in the Life of God*. New York: Alfred A. Knopf, 2001.

——. *God: A Biography*. New York: Alfred A. Knopf, 1995.

Niebuhr, H. Richard. *Christ & Culture*. New York: HarperCollins Publishers, 1951.

——. "The Grace of Doing Nothing." *The Christian Century*, March 23, 1932.

——. *The Kingdom of God in America*. Middletown, CT: Wesleyan University Press, 1988.

——. *The Social Sources of Denominationalism*. Whitefish, MT: Kessenger Publishing Co., 2004.

——. *The Responsible Self: An Essay in Christian Moral Philosophy*. Louisville: Westminster John Knox Press, 1999.

Niebuhr, Reinhold. *An Interpretation of Christian Ethics*. New York: Harper & Brothers, 1934.

——. *Beyond Tragedy: Essays on the Christian Interpretation of History*. New York: Scribner Books, 1979.

——. *The Irony of American History*. Chicago: University of Chicago Press, 1952/2008.

——. *Moral Man in Immoral Society: A Study of Ethics and Politics*. New York: Charles Scribner's Sons, 1934.

——. *The Nature and Destiny of Man: A Christian Interpretation—Human Nature*. Louisville: Westminster John Knox Press, 1941/1964.

——. "The Situation in the Middle East." *Christianity and Crisis* XVII (April 1957): 43.

Phillips, Kevin. *Bad Money: Reckless Finance, Failed Politics, and The Global Crisis of American Capitalism*. New York: Viking Penguin, 2008.

——. *American Theocracy: The Peril and Politics of Radical Religion, Oil, and Borrowed Money in the 21st Century*. New York: Viking Penguin, 2006.

——. *The Cousins' Wars: Religion, Politics, Civil Warfare, and the Triumph of Anglo-America*. New York: Basic Books, 1999.

Polkinghorne, John and Welker, Michael. *The End of the World and the Ends of God: Science and Theology on Eschatology*. Harrisburg, PA: Trinity Press International, 2000.

Polkinghorne, John. *The God of Hope and the End of the World*. New Haven: Yale University Press, 2003.

——. *Science and Creation: The Search for Understanding*. West Conshohochen, PA: Templeton Foundation Press, 2006.

Prejean, Helen. *Dead Man Walking: An Eyewitness Account of the Death Penalty in the United States*. New York: Vintage Books, 1993.

Rahner, Karl. "On the Theology of Hope." *A Rahner Reader*, ed. Gerald McCool. London: Darton, Longman & Todd, Ltd., 1975.

Ratzinger, Joseph and Habermas, Jürgen. *The Dialectic of Secularization: On Reason and Religion*. San Francisco: Ignatius Press, 2006.

Rauschenbusch, Walter. *Christianity and the Social Crisis of the 21st Century: The Classic That Woke Up the Church*, ed. Paul Rauschenbush. New York: HarperCollins Publishers, 2007.

Ruether, Rosemary R. *Gaia and God: An Ecofeminist Theology of Earth Healing*. New York: HarperCollins Publishers, 1992.

Samuelson, Robert J. *The Great Inflation and Its Aftermath: The Past and the Future of American Affluence*. New York: Random House, Inc., 2008.

Sen, Amartya. *Poverty and Famine: An Essay on Entitlement and Deprivation*. New York: Oxford University Press, Inc., 1981.

Shriver, Donald W. *An Ethic for Enemies: Forgiveness in Politics*. New York: Oxford University Press, Inc., 1995.

―――. *Rich Man, Poor Man: Christian Ethics for Modern Man*. Louisville: John Knox Press, 1972.

Simmel, Georg. *The Philosophy of Money*. New York: Routledge, 2004.

Smith, Adam. *The Wealth of Nations*, ed. Edwin Cannan. New York: Random House, Inc., 1994.

Spengler, Oswald et al. *The Decline of the West: An Abridged Edition*. New York: Oxford University Press, 1991.

Stackhouse, Max. *Christian Ethics and Economic Life*. Nashville: Abingdon, 1996.

Stark, Rodney. *Cities of God: The Real Story of How Christianity Became an Urban Movement and Conquered Rome*. New York: HarperOne, 2007.

Stiglitz, Joseph E. and Bilmes, Linda J. *The Three Trillion Dollar War: The True Cost of the Iraq Conflict*. New York: W.W. Norton & Company, Inc., 2008.

Stone, Ronald A. *Reinhold Niebuhr: Prophet to Politicians*. Lanham, MD: Rowman & Littlefield, 1983.

Tanner, Kathryn. *Economy of Grace*. Minneapolis: Augsburg Fortress, 2005.

Tawney, R.H. *Religion and the Rise of Capitalism*. Edison, NJ: Transaction Publishers, 1998.

Teilhard de Chardin, Pierre. *The Phenomenon of Man*, trans. Bernard Wall. New York: HarperCollins Publishers, Inc., 1975.

Torrance, David W. and Thomas F., eds. *Calvin's New Testament Commentaries*, 12 volumes. Grand Rapids: Eerdmans, 1960.

Toynbee, Arnold J. *A Study of History: Abridgement of Volumes I-VI*. New York: Oxford University Press, Inc. 1946/1974.

Vaux, Kenneth L. *Birth Ethics: Religious and Cultural Values in the Genesis of Life*. New York: Crossroads Publishing Company, 1989.

―――. *Death Ethics: Religious and Cultural Values in Prolonging and Ending Life*. New York: Continuum International Publishing Group, 1996.

―――. *Ethics and the War on Terrorism*. Eugene, OR: Wipf & Stock, 2002.

―――. *Powers That Make Us Human*. Urbana: University of Illinois Press, 1985.

―――. *Subduing the Cosmos: Cybernetics and Man's Future*. Louisville: John Knox Press, 1970.

Weber, Max. *The Protestant Ethic and the Spirit of Capitalism*. New York: Routledge Classics, 2001.

Weinberg, Steven. *The First Three Minutes: A Modern View of the Origin of the Universe*. New York: Basic Books, 1977/1988.

Wink, Walter. *Engaging the Powers: Discernment and Resistance in a World of Domination*. Minneapolis: Fortress, 1992.

―――. *Naming the Powers: The Language of Power in the New Testament*. Philadelphia: Fortress, 1984.

―――. *The Powers That Be: Theology for a New Millennium*. Minneapolis: Augsburg Fortress, 1998.

―――. *Unmasking the Powers: The Invisible Forces That Determine Human Existence*. Philadelphia: Fortress, 1986.

Yeo, Khiok-khng. "Your Humanity, Our Divinity." *Word Pictures of the New Testament: Color and Face of the Spirit*. Louisville: Westminster John Knox Press, forthcoming).